DESTINATION INDIA

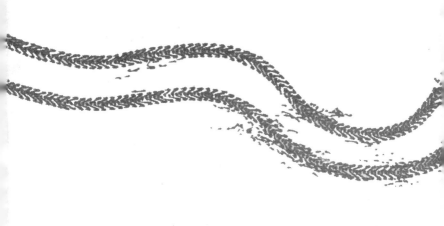

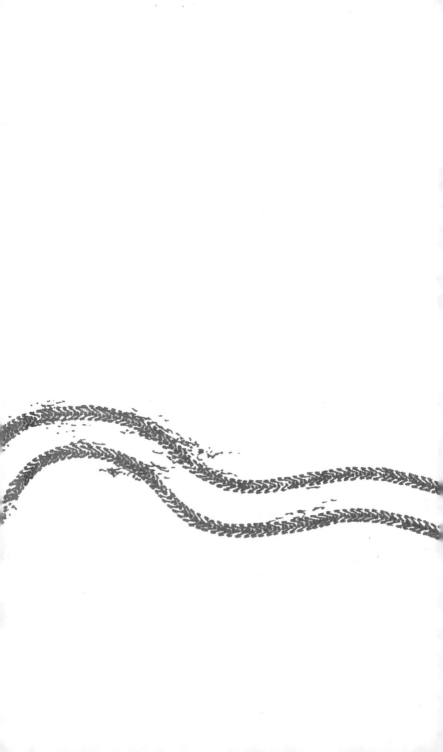

DESTINATION INDIA

FROM LONDON OVERLAND TO INDIA

and what we learned there

LLOYD I. RUDOLPH
SUSANNE HOEBER RUDOLPH

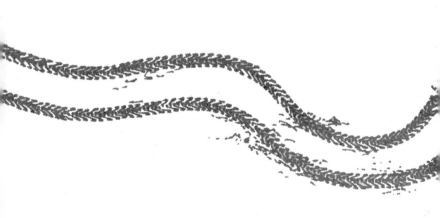

OXFORD

UNIVERSITY PRESS

OXFORD
UNIVERSITY PRESS

Oxford University Press is a department of the University of Oxford.
It furthers the University's objective of excellence in research, scholarship,
and education by publishing worldwide. Oxford is a registered trademark of
Oxford University Press in the UK and in certain other countries

Published in India by
Oxford University Press
YMCA Library Building, 1 Jai Singh Road, New Delhi 110 001, India

ISBN-13: 978-0-19-945055-8
ISBN-10: 0-19-945055-2

Typeset in Wiesbaden Swing 15/16 and Adobe Garamond Pro 10.5/16
by Sai Graphic Design, New Delhi 110055
Printed in India by Sapra Brothers, New Delhi 110092

Illustration (pp. i–iii) courtesy of Aniruddha De

This book is dedicated to our three children, now grown,
Jenny, Amelia, and Matthew.
They cheerfully accompanied us to India over the many years
we spent there and, like us, learned to appreciate India's
charms and challenges.

Contents

Introduction

Destination India is a book about why and how India came to occupy a central place in our imaginations and our lives. The opening chapter, "Travel Notes from Salzburg to Peshawar," tells the story of *getting there*. The year was 1956, the months July and August. Day by day and mile by mile, we recorded our impressions and experiences of people, landscapes, and encounters as we drove a 107-inch wheelbase Land Rover from London to Jaipur. Our 5,000-mile journey took us "East of Suez," across the ecological and cultural *limes* distinguishing Europe from Asia, and then over the Khyber into the Indian subcontinent.

As freshly minted PhDs, 26 and 28 years old, we were open to adventure and to knowledge of the Other. Funded by a Ford Foundation Foreign Area Training Fellowship, we found ourselves positioned at the cusp of the area studies era generated by the end of colonial rule.

The second chapter, "Writing India: A Career Overview,"[1] the first of the two chapters about *being there*, gives an analytic account of what we learned over five decades of teaching and writing about India, decades that included 11 research years in India.

The chapter starts with an argument in *The Modernity of Tradition*,[2] a book based on our first research year in India, that the then-regnant modernization theory was wrong in supposing that tradition would be swept into the dustbin of history and that "they" would become like "us." We showed how and why tradition was often adaptive, change dialectical, not dichotomous, and "we" could learn from "them."

The chapter goes on to highlight our main findings and arguments in the realm of ideas as they are found in our writing about social science inquiry and theory; the realm of institutions as they are found in our writing about state formation and institutional change; and in the realm of the public sphere as they are found in our writing about identity and policy.[3]

The third and concluding chapter, "The Imperialism of Categories: Situating Knowledge in a Globalizing World," discusses an important methodological lesson we learned from being there. Many Western scholars of "new nations" sought to find universal truths, truths that were said to be true everywhere and always. We found ourselves learning from the Other and grounding our concepts and categories in local knowledge and practice. We characterized our approach as situated knowledge, knowledge that arises out of particular times, places, and circumstances, and that results in contextual rather than universal truths.

Traveling through countries of Western Asia, Turkey, Iran, and Afghanistan, shaped our perspective. We learned that if India was less developed than the countries of Western Europe, it was more developed than the countries lying between Western Europe and South Asia.

From 1956–7 onward, roughly every fourth year until 1999–2000, we took leave to do research in India. In all, we spent 11 years on the subcontinent doing research. Starting with our second research year, 1962–3, the first of our three children accompanied us. Over the subsequent nine research years our children traveled to India with us. They attended Indian schools which included St Xavier's and Maharani Gayatri Devi Girls Public School in Jaipur, and the Woodstock School in Mussoorie/Landour. Living in India, they experienced Indian family life and formed lasting friendships. In the process, they acquired a passable Hindi. Beginning in 2001, as an aspect of our retirement arrangements, we have been able to spend the winter months, January through March, living and working in Jaipur.

At Harvard, where we did our PhDs in political science (Susanne 1955; Lloyd 1956) we studied comparative politics and nationalism with Samuel Beer, Rupert Emerson, and Carl Friedrich. We learned to analyze institutions, politics, and, even then, policy, as they were defined by European and American historical experience. Our graduate education at Harvard in the 1950s did not equip us, as our students at the University of Chicago were equipped from the 1960s onward, with knowledge of South Asian languages, history, and culture that the National Defense Education Act (NDEA), South Asia area, and language programs introduced by the Eisenhower administration in the post-Sputnik era made possible. We learned Hindi and about India's history, culture, and society on our own at home and while doing research in India.[4]

Our openness to area and language knowledge was partly a consequence of working while junior faculty at Harvard with David Riesman in his course on American character and social structure and with Erik Erikson in his course and seminar on life history and identity formation. These experiences prepared us intellectually and emotionally better than did our graduate education in political science to respond to living in and learning from India. They liberated us from the disciplinary straitjacket of political science and opened the way for us to be humanistic social scientists more concerned with meaning than with causation.

The title of our book, *Destination India*, has a literal and a figurative meaning. Literally it refers to the country, India, that captured our imagination as a place to encounter, study, and learn from; it refers to the country that we drove to overland from London in a Land Rover in order to be there; and the country that we spent 50 years studying, teaching, and writing about. Figuratively, *Destination India* becomes a trope for our academic career, for the 50 years we spent researching, theorizing, writing, and teaching about India. Our book tells the story of getting there and of being there.

Notes and References

1. "Writing India: A Career Overview" was first published in *India Review*, vol. 7, no. 4 (October–December 2008).

2. *The Modernity of Tradition: Political Development in India* (Chicago: University of Chicago Press, 1967).

3. For a detailed view of such scholarship, see our three-volume work, *Explaining Indian Democracy: A Fifty-year Perspective, 1956–2006* (New Delhi: Oxford University Press, 2008).

4. We were fortunate to be able to attend on several occasions Hindi language courses at the Landour Language School located in the Garhwal area of the lower Himalayas. Chitranjan Dutt, the Director, translated our first book on Gandhi, *Gandhi: The Traditional Roots of Charisma*, into Hindi for Orient Longman.

Travel Notes from
Salzburg to Peshawar

Previously published in the January–February 2013
edition of *The University of Chicago Magazine*.

Our trip diary was written under various conditions, some of them harsh. We jotted down the first half while the car was passing from one country to another on moderately respectable roads. But when we reached Persia, we could no longer write in the car — all our attention was devoted to keeping our stomachs below our lungs and not bumping our heads on the car ceiling. So the second half was written as we recuperated from the trip in Lahore, New Delhi, and even in Jaipur. The first part to page 16 turned out to be terse and stylistically a little threadbare. The part thereafter was done at greater leisure, and the interpretation may well have profited from that fact.

The notes start in Salzburg. We consider it the official starting point of our trip because we delayed in England and Germany along the way. Our vehicle was a new model of the

4   Land Rover, the 107-inch wheelbase, five-door station wagon which seats ten people and looks like an armored car meant for a battalion. It has ordinary front and rear seats, each of which accommodates three people, and two additional benches in the back that fold up against the sides of the car and accommodate two people each. The car is a blue-grey color with a white tropical roof set on top of the ordinary roof. Air circulates between the two layers, giving maximum cooling.

The car created some confusion wherever we went. In Germany, Sue's cousin Lars heard a speculating crowd put forward the theory that (a) it was an East German car and (b) it was meant for the new German Army. When we left England in the channel steamer, we found three otherwise sensible-looking custom officials flat on their backs beneath it. When we asked if we could be of assistance, they came out rather sheepishly and inquired if the car had four-wheel drive. We allowed that it had. This led to a lengthy conference as to whether the car could leave England — seems that all four-wheel drive vehicles are considered war goods. The matter was decided in our favor when we assured the officials that we didn't plan to visit Russia, and showed them the Ford Letter (with gold seal) which proclaimed that India — a Commonwealth country — was our destination.

In Turkey, the Army sentries saluted us with great regularity, and were always disconcerted when Sue smartly returned the salute. We had our doubts as to whether Rover could make it through Afghanistan. The King had recently ordered ten cars just like it for hunting expeditions, and we feared they'd think this was the first delivery.

The tires were heavy-duty truck style. Now, at the end of the trip, the two- to three-inch-deep two-layer tread has been smoothed to one-and-a-half inches — we were grateful for their depth. We carried a desert duty air filter, and mounted extra heavy springs. The four-wheel drive was supplemented by an additional set of gear ratios beginning below first gear — when necessary, Rover could inch along either up or down a very steep hill so that one could barely see him move, and could hold him in maximum control. The extra gear ratios delivered enormous power to front and rear wheels, so that there were few places Rover couldn't conquer.

He was crisis-tested by one of Sue's intrepid German uncles, Herbert Fischer, who took him into the rain-soaked, muddy Fischer forest near Hanover to see if he could get out again. While we sat in the back chewing our nails and fearing for Rover's life, Herbert happily sought out mires into which he plunged up to the axle, ruts, steep places, foot-deep potholes and other inconvenient nooks. Rover came through triumphantly. Only when the ordeal was over and we were backing out of the worst road we had tried did disaster strike. Rover's front left wheel slipped off the rather steep slope on the left, and gently settled in a bog of fallen leaves, mud and spring water.

We were desolate. For two hours Herbert, Lloyd, Sue, cousin Britta and Gunther Fischer, Sue's uncle from Fröndenberg, labored to build a stone road under the settling wheel, but to no avail. Finally, to the immense satisfaction of the Westphalian farmers who had shaken their heads with misgivings when they saw us move into the forest, we had to get a horse. The big, 15 zentner beast pulled us out in 10 seconds without batting an eyelash. We are happy to say that the conditions in the Fischer forest were really crisis conditions. We never met such difficulties again until we arrived in Rajasthan, where two bullocks and eight men once had to do what one horse did in Germany.

We had not expected to drive all the way when we arrived in Europe. The thought had been with us for a year, but we felt it would take too long and prove to be grueling. But the assurance of a pretty Indian lady in the London tourist office, that people had been known to make the trip in 24 days, and the sight of our vehicle — it was much bigger than the one we had ordered, due to a snafu at Continental Motors in Boston — persuaded us to think about the trip again. We procured Iranian and Afghan visas in one hectic day in London, and the Yugoslav visa in one morning at Bonn. So we turned back our tickets on the Asia, wrote Stan Miles that we couldn't meet him in Rome and Naples, and made plans to equip ourselves for the trip.

We bought all our provisions in Düsseldorf and Salzburg, a good policy because prices there are much better than in the States. Bedding, cookery and all equipment cost us approximately $60. In case anyone wants to take such a trip, our shopping list is given in Appendix I.

Before leaving Düsseldorf, Sue spent an evening with Marlies Trömel running up curtains on Marlies' sewing machine. These we strung up on a thin nylon line which we secured under the bolts above the window corner. During the day, we pushed the curtains back and tied them with string; at night they covered the windows on three sides. On the fourth side, in front, we hung up our clothes on hangers from the ceiling, giving us complete privacy.

The Rover made up into a bed. The second seat flattened out, the back of the front seat was laid across the back benches, and the cushions from the front seats made headrests. Cousins Britta and Lars, who tested the bed one night in Kuindorf, found it uncomfortable, but with some improvements initiated by Uncle Herbert we learned to love it.

Since we carried all our luggage with us, we had to transfer it out of the back of the car into the front seat each night before we could make up the bed. We routinized this process enough so that it became quite simple. Lloyd usually made the transfer, made the bed, and put on sheets, pillows and blankets while Sue prepared the supper.

For cooking, we had a Higgins two-burner gas stove, which we set just inside the door in the rear of the car when we cooked. For breakfast and supper we put up our little wooden table and folding chairs, set the table with paper napkins and the plastic dishes, and tried to keep a gently civilized routine. As long as we were in wine-producing countries we generally had wine for dinner. Thereafter, we switched to hot tea.

After dinner, we washed dishes in hot, soapy water in our folding rubber dish-pan, sometimes washed out a few clothes and hung them on a line tied to a nearby tree. In the mornings, while Sue cooked breakfast, Lloyd propped his mirror on the spare tire which was screwed on top of the hood, perched the pot with hot shaving water on the fender and shaved. Keeping house on the road was always some trouble. But it refreshed and strengthened us as no hotel stay ever did. We're not quite sure why this was so, but we think the manipulation of household equipment gave us the sense of being more than mere rootless wanderers upon the face of the earth.

The vital statistics of the trip are as follows: we left Salzburg on July 26 and arrived in Peshawar on August 20, a matter of 25 days. The mileage from Salzburg to Peshawar

Land Rover at Kuindorf, Westphalia, Germany, Susanne's maternal family's home, being washed on way to India, July 1956. Susanne stands at rear and her cousin, Britta Fischer, at the front.

was 5114 miles, and the cost of the trip itself, excluding all pre-trip expenses, was about $300. The pre-trip expenses incurred because we wanted to make the trip by car came to another $384 — although we would have incurred $250 of this amount (insurance premium for the car) in any case as soon as we decided to take a car to India. Anyone who is interested in the details of our cost-accounting may look at Appendix II which lists pre-trip expenses, and Appendix III which gives a breakdown by country and by expenditure topic of our expenses.

We were amazed, when we finished the trip, at the low total cost of gasoline (about $113). We had expected to pay an average of $.60 per gallon throughout the Middle East, but actual prices ranged from approximately $.25 in Turkey (assuming black market exchange rates) to $.40 in Afghanistan. (In spite of what Time International Edition of September 17 says about $.75 gas in Afghanistan.)

We should point out that such a trip is an enormously rewarding experience for the strong of limb and stout of heart. The difficulties which loom so large when one hears about the trip become rather small things when one meets them, annoying, perhaps frustrating, but not frightening. Camping all the way probably involves the same risks as camping along a US highway. That too is not entirely safe, certainly less safe than the National Parks. There is always the possibility that one may encounter the one or two criminal souls in every area along the way, but it is not an immediate possibility. The fact that everything is new and strange and possibly threatening creates a chronic underlying strain, a fear of the unknown which one must learn to live with. Such a trip is a calculated risk. But anyone who is in good physical condition, with a balanced psyche, a good car, a bit of luck, and a capacity to improvise can make the trip. We have no general rules or recommendations for people who want to try it. Meeting difficulties along the way is a personal ad hoc process which everyone has to work out for himself. What follows is an account of how we did it.

July 26

Did big laundry on glorious sunny morning at camp outside Salzburg. All the laundry accumulated on the drive down through Germany. Sue reveling in domesticity, Lloyd champing at the bit. Drove into Salzburg with laundry triumphantly flopping on nylon laundry lines in back of car. Money for which we'd been waiting for three days finally came. Moral — never carry your money in American bank drafts. Negotiable only after expensive, time-consuming cable exchange. Cable came just before noon. Ate some kuchen and coffee to celebrate. With Schlagsahne. Did some more quick shopping. Salzburg shops wonderful. Many tempting things. Bought some land-jäger for emergencies, piece of good bacon for outdoor breakfast, peaches, tomato, butter. Off at two for Graz.

Between 2 and 6:30, when we made camp, we drove through most of the Salzkammergut, with its breathtaking views, splendid mountains, and unbelievably green snow-fed lakes.

Contemplated the cool azure waters, which seem underlaid by white, against dark-green mountains at St. Gilgen. Decided good place for summer vacation some more restful year. Many Zimmer frei in unpretentious houses in this area.

Camped in field belonging to an inn at the foot of a mountain. Nice, simple, rural inn; owned horses, pigs. Somebody did something dreadful to those pigs — deathly pork noises much of the night. Very cold in car. Rose before sun-topped mountains. Very cold. Bundled up in sweaters until sun-capped mountain tops when temperature became quite comfortable.

July 27

Spent morning in Graz buying Dinar, replacing Sue's lost sunglasses. Graz already a little less like Western Europe. Women, houses look different. Police still as nice as all the Austrian police we met. Bought some eggs. One turned out to be rotten. Bought some Weichsel — soft sort of sour cherry. Very thirst-quenching on the long, warm drive.

Austrians, at least in the rural districts, have a language of their own: Kassa (Kasse); bassiert (gerieben); I (Ich). We liked Austria very much. Visceral reaction to people favorable (and all our reactions on this trip were visceral — a rational, intellectual assessment is difficult when one lives off the country and meets people only fleetingly), blue eyes, nice reddish-brown mountain tan; off-hand sort of competence.

Crossed Yugoslavian border around 2. Had to declare things like cameras, etc. The officials looked around in the car, had us open one freshly wrapped package which contained mounts for slides. No trouble. Fatherly-type customs officer. Reminded Lloyd of Colonel Henry. At border met German in Mercedes who had just come from Teheran in one week (in retrospect, we think this is an unlikely story). He gave us a map of Turkey, and some tips on road conditions.

At the border we picked up Anshen (?), a Norwegian medical student bound for Zagreb. Nice fellow, but excessively anxious to educate us. "Soon we will see children," he lectured, "with bellies that are round not because they are healthy, but because they are hungry. For you see, hunger does not always make people thin, it may bloat their stomachs." Or, "You know you cannot trust all the water in countries outside Europe."

A little out of Maribor we had to take a 15—20 kilometer detour, which was all to the good because it took us into some lovely hills where wine grew on all the southern slopes. Many shrines — Christ on the Cross at every turning of the road — the most agonized Christ figures either of us had ever seen. We thought we found an inverse ratio, in that part of Yugoslavia, between Christs on Crosses and party and national flags.

On the way toward Zagreb we came through Friday eve-ning festivities. Truckloads of country people coming together at an inn garden near Narazdin — violins, dancing, and beer. The Army, which we found in evidence throughout the country, also on the road in companies on trucks. To get through the crowds on the roads, the truck beeped furiously, and we soon followed behind, also tooting noisily and happily. July 28, we later found out, is the date on which the old Croatian government was replaced by the present one, and celebration was already beginning.

The road from Maribor over Narazdin to Zagreb was asphalt, except for the detour. But speed was hardly possible: the haying all seemed to be finished just that afternoon and evening, and the horse-drawn hay wagons added to the confusion on the roads. But chickens were the greatest road hazard, particularly the indeterminate fellows who changed their minds in the middle of the road and erratically sought to exterminate themselves under our swerving wheels. Everybody who walked the road had a pitch fork, man, woman and child. Women didn't seem to possess shoes in this area, though the men did. We saw more corn being grown here than we had since the US.

The area toward Zagreb compares somewhat with the last, pre-border part of Austria — stucco houses without fresh stucco, dun-colored. The people look rather heavy-hearted, stolid, but all the children wave when you pass. Cars are rather an oddity and an event on the roads. Consequently we had it mostly to ourselves as far as motorized traffic went. We felt conspicuously well-off, though God only knows we were no fashionable sight in our dusty looking vehicle and ditto clothes. (Whatever sense of guilt we labored under blunted very swiftly — by the time we arrived in India, we had acquired a sense of Sahib-ness.)

We camped at 8 or so off the road in a harvested field, after inquiring of some passing farmers if anyone was likely to mind. Anshen rolled up in his sleeping bag near us. The hay wagons and truckloads of soldiers rumbled by most of the night, but we slept well.

July 28

Spent the morning in Zagreb at the Volkswagen Service Garage trying to get screens made for our car windows. We were troubled at the prospect of mosquitoes particularly in malarial areas. We had no nets and to keep the car windows closed at night would surely become impossible further south. The Volkswagen Garage was new but rather pathetic. Lloyd, who investigated the place from end to end, reported that there was absolutely no equipment except hand tools in the huge structure.

A German-speaking mechanic was assigned to our job. He proposed to fix screening to metal frames and fasten the frames to our windows. He spent an hour with us driving around trying to locate metal screws, but found none. He then promised to fix the frames and screens anyway, and locate the screws to attach them to our car that afternoon. He complained bitterly from a sense of frustrated craftsmanship: "We cannot get the tools and materials to do a proper job, and get paid nothing on top of it." When we returned for the frames in the afternoon, they had been badly put together with sloppy workmanship for which the lack of equipment was not sufficient excuse. The metal screws were not produced — "You will certainly find them in Belgrade!" We never did find them, but then we had little trouble with mosquitoes. To finish the tale, the screens rusted away in a few

days. The adventure cost us 2000 dinar (about $6) — and a
half a day.

Meanwhile we shopped in the Zagreb main square, for
bread, wine, sausage and a water bottle. The latter, which served
us through Persia, was a large green one in a basket covering. It
held ten liters, and provided baths and dishwater in plenty each
day. We asked a passing housewife about bread (in German).
She took us to the shop and guided our purchase, was delighted
to hear we were from the US (a happier land!) and could
hardly bring herself to leave us.

In the shop where we purchased two bottles of a nice domestic
white wine, the manager embarrassed us by insisting on serving
us before a lot of obviously lower-class women in babushkas.
We ate a poor lunch at an outdoor restaurant with doubtful
tablecloths, ordering with the aid of two young Italian-speaking
Yugoslavs who were obviously bohème types, one in a dashing,
brightly colored striped shirt and shorts, and a smart little
beard.

We left Zagreb around 3 o'clock on the Autoput. It is a
wide road with one lane in each direction, quite enough for high
speeds when so very few cars travel the road. Toward evening
we arrived at one of several rest stations established by the
government since the war. The spacious dining room had a large
and elaborate free-form design of white mosaic set in black. It
was clearly influenced by a certain heavy-handed modernism that
prevails in some western nightclubs. The setting was pleasant,
however, and we enjoyed a cooling gespritzer and some light

food. Among the others in the restaurant were two carloads of attractive young French men and women Istanbul–bound, but we were too tired to strike up an acquaintance.

We very much wanted a shower. The manager, who was struggling to live up to the cosmopolitan status to which his establishment aspired, but going under instead in a sea of forms and passports and detail, personally and proudly showed us bathrooms, upstairs terrace, and bedroom. Our bedroom was clean and pleasant, with a little porch opening off the solid wall of windows on the east side. The enormous upstairs terrace had a splendid view of the fuel pumps, and the water in the shower stopped working just after Lloyd has soaped up, but when the moon came out the terrace became lovely, and the manager got the water working within ten minutes. We had a pleasant stay.

July 29

Autoput remained splendid to Belgrade. From Belgrade to Svetozarevo the road was curvaceous and hilly but smooth and well maintained. After Cupriyo, a rough sort of stone and gravel composition that became worse further south accompanied us. We could go no more than 25 mph on it. It was a catastrophe to be passed on this road. The clouds didn't settle until half a mile behind the passing vehicle — one had the choice of closing the window and steaming, or opening it and being embalmed in dust.

On the road signs NIS, the next major city, began to be spelled HИN, with the N turned the wrong way around. We learned the Cyrillic alphabet from necessity, with the aid of a map which foresightedly gave that alphabet in the margin.

The country varied as we went along. Outside Belgrade is lovely, rather hilly country. As we went south, it became flatter, and though farmed everywhere, it seemed poorer. Houses with red tile roofs dotted the landscape. At lunch we had company — a boy, perhaps seven years old, in a little pair of patched cotton short pants. He carried a glass jug and a cup, and was on his way to the well when he met us. He sat down nearby and quietly watched our arrangements with great interest. Every now and then he would make sympathetic noises, i.e. when a sausage escaped and dropped into the freshly prepared tea. We indicated to him that we were Americans, and to make the concept understandable, we pointed to him and said, "Yugoslav." This brought a vigorous response: much shaking of the head and a strong affirmation — "Serbia." This happened several times in the country south of Beograd; men who stopped to peer into our pot and watch the machinations with the stove all identified themselves as Serbians if we got to the matter of national identification.

Nis, which has a splendid walled city within a city, was almost a ghost town when we passed through it. It was Sunday, everything was closed — including the rather magnificent, often apparently functionless buildings with which all the larger Yugoslavian towns are equipped. The otherwise quiet streets were full of soldiers, all looking for something to do. We failed to find any restaurants that we could bring ourselves to go into, although we got gasoline by following Benzin signs to a little side street where the mechanic was listening to French love songs on his radio. A radio!

As we left town, we passed a small convoy of Yugoslav army trucks. When this same convoy repassed us on the dusty road to Skopje, where we were trying to eat dinner while keeping the dust out of the stew, it had grown. Some thirty or more trucks passed us.

We camped off the Skopje road in a nice field — cool and pleasant.

July 30

Woke up at 5:30. Everybody on the way to Monday morning market. Women with quacking ducks in their baskets, clean white cloths over their heads with roses pinned on. Bullocks, calves, tomatoes, peppers, all on the way to the market. Having no fix- ings for breakfast, we followed the crowd, after a lengthy discus- sion with a passing farmer who offered Lloyd a cigarette from a silver cigarette case. Men here wear wooly shakos, sleeveless sheep-skin jackets with the skin side out, dark Jodphur style trousers ballooning at the thigh and tight at the calf. Further south toward Skopje and beyond, we saw men in white, loose shirts and trousers, belted in black wool and sometimes with short wool, bolero-style jackets. As we headed south during the day, the farmland decreased and the herding of sheep increased. Finally, as we came out of the relatively flat farmland of Serbia into the arid, wild and lonesome hill country of Macedonia, even sheep became rare.

In Skopje, another one of these Yugoslavian cities that lack the conviction of being cities, we had doubtful, greasy, saturated sweet pastry. Lloyd ate servings of ice-cream, after being assured by Sue that if the result was disastrous no sympathy would be extended. No ill effects!

Skopje was very hot. As in all Yugoslavian cities, very few cars populated the rather wide streets. A lonesome cop in the large main square directed a desultory cyclist, one or two ladies in Turkish trousers (Skopje belongs to the East almost as much to the West), a lone car. The Post Office gave the same impression of make-believe. Behind its many-pillared facade lay a large hall with many large glass doors, each of which promised many things beyond in Cyrillic and French. One door promised more than the others, and we entered it. No one there. Inside appeared some twenty opaque glass counter windows. We chose one, approached it warily, saw no one, peered over the top and discovered that there was no one behind any of the counters. The chairs had been turned up-side down on the tables, and the room had a deserted aspect. We went out into the hall again, and tried another glass door, with a more modest legend. This time we were successful. One of six or eight counters was going. Behind it sat a stringy, sensible-looking lady, who sold us stamps for Airmail postcards to the US. When one of the stamps would not stick, she brought out a methodical little gluepot and proceeded to give each stamp an individual gluing.

Here, as everywhere in Yugoslavia, we muddled through in German, but only after inquiring first if the other person spoke English, to establish that we were not ourselves Germans. Germans are not too well loved in some of the rural districts where the resistance movement was strong, and we had need of local approval as campers. Speaking of local approval — we were told at the border to register with the police at every town where we stayed. Since we never stayed in a town, we never registered, except at the restaurant on the Autoput.

But to go back to the big joy of the day, the small market at Leskovac. Our arrival there created a great sensation. We took some pictures, creating more sensation. We then undertook to purchase eggs, tomatoes and two little pottery cups. At each purchase, there was a great coming together of viewers. The eggs were quoted at six for 72 dinar, but Lloyd only had a 500 dinar note ($1.25). This created consternation, for the egg lady had no change, but a quiet man in a better-quality shirt detached himself from the crowd and made change, while twenty eyes watched intently. The process was repeated at the stand of the tomato lad who sold to us at 20 dinar for the pound. The crowd had meanwhile increased, including two soldiers and the rest farmers. We went on to the cups.

Sue picked up two cups, asked "Dinar?" The man replied "Zwanzig." Lloyd pulled out a twenty dinar note. Meanwhile some discussion stirred the crowd and when Lloyd offered the note, the man indicated that each cup was twenty dinar. Sue decided the crowd had raised the price on the foreign tourists, and assumed a bargaining posture. The potter looked uncertain — he was obviously being pushed by the crowd to stick at 40. Sue put down the cups. The potter looked unhappy. Lloyd then offered him 30, and the bargain was closed.

Later we did some arithmetic: 40 dinar are 10 cents. Sue felt silly. All this rot about the foreigner getting stuck by local bargainer — we could have afforded the $.10 easily enough.

Our impressions of Macedonia: this is a wild, arid, hilly land. The scrub on the hillsides barely seems to survive. A very hot afternoon on dusty, rough winding roads shook our stomachs up pretty badly, and taught us that a long stretch on rugged roads produces a vague, general malaise. If the roads had been better, we might have had greater appreciation for the drama of those hills, which are a little reminiscent of north English hills.

Total impressions of Yugoslavia: this is a poor country. (It would have appeared much less so had we arrived here from the other direction.) It is still predominantly rural and unmechanized — we saw six tractors and no other mechanized farm equipment. Of the tractors, one was on demonstration, two on construction jobs, and three on farms. The rural people seemed cheerful, particularly in Serbia. In Croatia, they looked more sullen, waved less. But these are rather swift, visceral reactions. Much of the country is very pretty — the bottomlands along the Autoput with their luscious swamp growth and water birds, the green farmland of Serbia, and even the dry hills of Macedonia where only sunflowers grow in large fields. We were sorry we missed the coast which is said to be most beautiful.

We made a point of looking at goods in the Yugoslavian shops. They are well stocked for ordinary needs of a simple life — pots, pans, bottles, cloths, etc. But for the bourgeois life — even a modest one — they are not well stocked. Shoes are expensive and quite without style. Very, very few people look neat and well dressed in a middle class sense, although the rural people dress neatly and appropriately. We didn't become aware of how poorly the white collar types looked until we arrived in Greece and saw the men in the cities and some in the villages in their clean, white, freshly pressed open-collar shirts and freshly whitened shoes. (India, too, when we arrived there, displayed a more respectable looking petty bourgeoisie than Yugoslavia.) Though we saw exceptions, the overall impression in Yugoslavia was that ironing boards and pure colors didn't exist — every one in the cities had a drab, unironed look. This applied to the army as well. The officers often looked snappy, but the quality of enlisted uniforms — of pale green, poor quality cotton — and the way they were maintained was rather amateurish. We saw the army everywhere — every town had an installation of some sort.

While the Yugoslavs were on the whole nice to us, and the country was lovely in many places, we felt somehow relieved to arrive in Greece. We arrived at the border in the evening, and reveled in a dinner at the fancy customs-house restaurant, the first we had enjoyed since the Autoput. As we continued into Greece in the night, we were struck by the fact that large har- vesting machines were everywhere, working through the night by electricity, a sight we never saw in Yugoslavia. Greek national habits, or perhaps her capitalism, make it a less drab, a gayer land than Yugoslavia.

On the way toward Thessaloniki, we began to encounter a strange phenomenon, so strange that we thought we'd had too long a day of it. Small trees moved silently across the road in front of us. Huge bushes slowly growled down the highway toward us. Agitated flora enlivened the road sides. The bushes, we eventually realized, were heavily camouflaged troop transports with their lights out, the lively greenery camouflaged men. We, of course, had our lights shining brightly, as indeed was essential if we were not to annihilate a donkey and his guide every ten yards. But the transports became more frequent, their drivers signaled to us to put down our lights, and eventually an armed sentry stepped into the road and halted us. For five minutes before that, we had been reviewing the recent history of Greco-Yugoslavian relations, and theorizing that the Yugoslavian troop movements we had seen on the other side of the border and the Greek troops we saw on the move now might have some mutually antagonistic aim. But our sentry, who made us pull off the road and join a group of donkeys, farmers, and Italian motorcyclists, which he had already collected there, quickly eased our minds. War games, big ones, and ones to which Turkey and England had, incidentally, not been invited.

Our detainer spoke French and had studied Political Science at the University of Athens. He and his colleagues fed us and the Italian motorcyclists fresh watermelon, and when we got tired of waiting after an hour and proposed to park somewhere and spend the night, they found a place for us behind their own bivouac.

July 31

The morning hours in Thessaloniki, where we arrived at 9 a.m., were splendid. We sat in Floca Brother's coffeehouse and drank coffee and ate croissants with jam, and caught up on the sinking of the Andrea Doria and the nationalization of the Suez Canal. Thessaloniki is a city of over half a million, we heard. Here we began to meet the open, streetside shops on narrow streets which continued with us in many forms for the rest of the trip. Brasses and copper and tin pots everywhere; the blacksmith shop's pounding can be heard at a distance, and the tailor bends over his Pfaff machine a few feet from where the horses pass.

The language by which we got along in Greece was French. Anyone who had a somewhat advanced education — and in villages you could usually spot them by their white collar appearance — had some French in school.

We left Thessaloniki about 10 a.m., and drove to Alexandropolis by 8 p.m. In the meantime, we made the extensive acquaintance of the Greek police — a snappy corps, with their well-kept green uniforms and uniformly large black mustaches. Throughout Greece, on the highways we drove, they have little sentry-like boxes at perhaps 50 mile intervals. At about 1 o'clock, a mile outside the beautiful city of Avalla on the Aegean, we were arrested at one of these stations. But the arrest soon deteriorated into absurdity: no one could communicate the charge to us. We were not too dismayed, because we had good consciences, plus a new psychological protection which we had imperceptibly acquired on the way East — a totally irrational confidence that we're Americans-and-you'd-better-not-try-to-give-us-any-unreasonable-difficulties. We think that this rather unexpected new self-confidence is the psychological counterpart for what sustained the British in so many unequal situations.

In any case, our policemen, not being able to communicate with us, called in a passing army officer for consultation. The officer was no help, but he used the word Russki frequently enough that we tentatively concluded this had something to do with (a) last night's maneuvers and (b) we were suspected of being Russkis, spying no doubt. This impression was confirmed when the policeman got into our car and asked us to proceed to a nearby army encampment. Our unexpected arrival there occasioned a great buttoning up and straightening out among troops who had a right to expect freedom from females in their noonday off-hour in this out-of-the-way camp.

A few moments later a non-commissioned officer emerged from one of the red, corrugated iron quonset huts that sat among the trees. He, it turned out, spoke English, and informed us that we were charged with killing a cow with our car. Someone had seen us do it, and taken down our number.

The long and the short of this story is: it wasn't a cow, it was a horse, and we didn't do it. Fortunately we saw the accident, or the confusion would have lasted much longer. The horse had run into the path of a defenseless Volkswagen, knocking in its (the W's) nose and one light, and killing itself (the horse). We stopped to see if we could help, because we had met the Iranian driver and his young German bride at the Greek customs, where they were completely searched. (We were not searched at all. It was a spot check.) While we were explaining this story to the police, the V.W. drove up, looking duly bashed. The Iranian, one of the tensest men we have ever met, was all for telling the police that his wife was pregnant with quintuplets and they couldn't stay to answer questions, but his calmer wife dissuaded him. We translated their story to our interpreter who translated to the police. When we last saw them, they were returning to the site of the act, where they were to argue their case before the local police. We felt sorry for them — it would be awkward arguing with an irate Greek farmer and the Greek police in German and Persian.

We arrived in Alexandropolis via worsening roads, after dark, in time to see people flocking the main streets in the evening cool. The city seemed very provincial — little vehicular traffic, etc., but people were well dressed.

We ate at a sidewalk cafe — some liver and veal dish — we drank beer and chatted with three Germans, two men and a woman, who were on their way to Istanbul to join the branch office of Luft-Hansa there. We bedded down just outside town in a field at 11:30, happily remembering the beautiful view of the Aegean which we had from the high hills that afternoon.

Left for Istanbul at 7 a.m., after breakfast and big laundry. Under these conditions, we returned to the old technique of boiling laundry to get it white. The day was grueling. The road deteriorated going East, a silent testimony to the infrequency of Turko-Greek contacts, becoming dustier, holier, curvier, hotter. It did not, as we were told in Alexandropolis, consist of a river bed, but it was bad enough. We passed through Turkish customs around noon, without much time or difficulty. People along the road on the Turkish side didn't look confidence-inspiring, but rather shifty and cheerless. There was a lot of peering but no waving. At Edirne, we saw some lovely Mosques, and took some pictures. We were determined to reach Istanbul that day, and made good time on what asphalt roads there were. Everywhere in Turkey, but especially outside Istanbul, we saw extensive evidence of a large road-building program, probably part of the program which is helping along the country's raging inflation. A lot of good heavy equipment, possibly bought with American aid funds, was in use on the roads. If the present pace is kept up, Turkey should have one of the best road systems in the East very soon.

In Istanbul, where we arrived exhausted and dusty, we spent an hour finding a hotel. We wanted to stay at the magnificent Istanbul Hilton, which, provided one changes one's money at black-market rates, is quite reasonable. But the Hilton was quite full. So were the Divan Oteli, the Park Hotel and the

Pera Palas. We finally located the Pierre Loti, on the old city side of the Golden Horn. The hotel manager spoke a doubt-ful French, his rooms were decent, the food all right, and the bathrooms not too clean.

August 2

Our missions in Istanbul were three: to service Rover, to buy some Turkish money (we had none so far), and to see something of the city. After a breakfast of bread, butter, and something that may have been honey, we set out on the adventure of cashing our traveler's checks. We were equipped with the knowledge that official rates were 2.80 lira to the dollar, and the unofficial ranged from 6 to 9 lira. Our problem was that we were strange to the city, and the banks would give only the official rate. We had been told that usually someone at the hotel would offer to facilitate exchange, but no amount of insinuating voiced inqui-ries at the Pierre Loti brought any results. We knew that the Hilton readily accepted payment of bills at 6—1 rate, but that was no help to us.

Open-faced types that we are, we trotted ourselves inno-cently to American Express and asked to change our checks. When they quoted the official rate, we asked where the grey market was to be found, please. We received the cool, official expression of ignorance that our dumb question asked for. We then tried a Turkish bank, with the same result.

Since Rover had to be serviced, we discontinued exchange chasing for a bit and delivered him to a garage on the Marmok

Caddesi which the Matas Ticari Trading Corporation had
recommended. An executive of the Corporation, Mr. Hanaman
(?), came over to translate for us and gave swift instruction
to a slim, mustachioed mechanic squatting near us in the dusty
little office of the garage. Rovers are used by all the police in
Istanbul, so the garage was very busy. But our vehicle received
prompt attention.

We asked Mr. Hanaman about the money situation. While
he made it clear that he couldn't help us, he suggested that the
US Consul might. That's what they had told us at American
Express in Salzburg, and accounted for our unpreparedness.
We asked him about the legal situation, since we understood the
money market was more grey than black. "The legal situation,"
he said, "is: how much money did you declare when you came
in?" He drove us to the consulate, where we were told by the
secretary that she couldn't tell us where to get money except on
the free market at Beyrut. "Thank you," we said, "that's too
far." A personage in the hall whom Lloyd accosted told us that
we should check with the military attaché's office. We got the
impression that they put in lira at favorable rates of exchange
for the military personnel. But when we spoke to the sergeant
there, he allowed that he could just get enough to take care of
his own people.

We then decided to try our last resort, Captain Cellijan,
whom Lloyd met at the AG [Adjutant General] school at Fort
Benjamin Harrison. The sergeant at the Consulate thought we
might be able to trace his whereabouts at First Army (Turk)

Headquarters. Since we still had no money, and now no car, we walked over, down some of the busy narrow streets, to Taksim square — the Times Square of Istanbul — past the statue of Ataturk — he appears everywhere. In busts, on rearing horseback, on pictures on the wall in a stiff, turndown collar and formal clothes, in uniform, always with a firm expression on his thin-lipped mouth and his long, squared face. We walked up the tree-lined boulevard that leads past the park where the band plays in the late afternoon and where small and middle sized boys play a kind of soccer on the white stone terrace overlooking the lawn.

The ladies on the streets of Istanbul include an extraordinary number of slim, full-bosomed, well-built women, many of them beautiful and quietly sultry. We saw a number of young women wearing long, thick braids and looking the sultrier for the innocent hairdo. In the country one can't judge the women so well because they wear voluminous shawls and are still rather retiring. The men are less obviously outstanding and attractive, and the rural practice, also seen in urban centers, of keeping a three day's growth of beard does not endear them to the female eye. We saw no veils on women or special hats on men in Istanbul. All except visiting country folk wear the modern dress.

The traffic here is very thick, and the trolleys carry crowds of people including always a contingent of five or six little boys who jump on the back and hold on to god-only-knows-what with their bare toes and hands. The Istanbul police wear snappy white coats (wool!) and blue trousers, and are very helpful. As far as traffic in Turkey in general is concerned, there are many American cars in the big cities, and some in the country. People rely on brakes rather than on a generally accepted conception of the right of way. Lloyd was always fit to be tied after an hour's driving in any city. In the provincial towns the automobile has not yet received recognition of its rights on a par with cows, donkeys, people and other users of the right of way. Lloyd always sat on the horn in small towns, but usually people, whether walking toward or away from you, would still look up with surprise when you gently nudged them with the fender, though you had been beeping for several minutes.

We still haven't killed a chicken — a truly glorious record. Anyhow, there we were on the way to 1st Army Headquarters. We continued past the fancy hotels to a large, once-magnificent yellowish building, now in an advanced state of disrepair, and entered the building from the back, past guards with fixed bayonets. Inside, we found dark, rough hewn, worn floorboards, peeling walls, a feel of wood and soot, old stucco and a sour smell. A guard, to whom we had communicated our desire to find the American APO (to find an interpreter who could in turn help us find Captain Cellijan), led us up a broad, dusty, winding staircase and down a long hall. Inside, we found the Americans out to lunch; the interpreters were in, and told us no one in any office would be back before 1:30. Sue was very depressed, convinced we'd never find Cellijan, sneezing from a bad cold, bemoaning the lack of Turkish currency, the late lunch, and life in general. Lloyd displayed a moderate optimism, and we waited.

Finally the sergeant arrived, a big, heavy man who looked like a sergeant should. Lloyd made cautious inquiries concerning currency, and the sergeant immediately opened negotiations with the Turkish interpreters. The negotiations involved numerous phone calls, some muffled conferring, and finally an offer: $50-worth of travelers checks changed at 6—1. Life immediately perked up. We ate lunch at the Divan Oteli, with three waiters and clean table cloths to reward ourselves for the long wait.

Before leaving the Army Headquarters, we made one attempt to find Captain C., but only a desultory one now that the money was in hand. Our interpreter told us that one room in the headquarters building is the place where Ataturk studied to be a reserve officer when the building was a reserve training school. But we never did find Cellijan.

After lunch, we ran over to the American Consulate dispensary in search of halizone pills and potassium permanganate and some lozenges for Sue's throat. A nice American lady who found us standing baffled before the dispensary, closed for the third time that day, gave us her halizone pills, and took us in her Chevy to a pharmacy for the other things. Then we shopped for other odds and ends, and went home, exhausted. Even the Pierre Loti looked comforting then.

August 3

Today we drove from Istanbul to a place this side of Ankara. Toward evening we found a pretty willow grove by a stream.

We talked with a friendly farmer who was washing the wheels
of his oxcart at our stream, while his veiled wife lurked in the
background. He indicated that he was but a simple man pointing at his disintegrating waist-coat, and did not have much
here — pointing to his head — compared to academic types like
ourselves. Slept well. Did another laundry.

August 4

On to Ankara. Sue was feeling very badly with her cold, and
didn't appreciate the arid dusty nowhere in the midst of which
Ankara sits. The city itself is very attractive with its parks,
boulevards, and public monuments.

We needed more money, but the attempt to get a good
exchange at the Park Hotel restaurant failed utterly. No one
had ever heard of any exchange other than 2.80 to 1. We finally
succeeded with the MP at the US embassy, who was on his
way back to the States and wanted some dollars. We mailed a
batch of postcards with the aid of a nice little English-speaking
fellow who led us through the maze at the post office.

At four in the afternoon we plunged back into the forbidding,
arid country. No appealing campsites appeared anywhere, and
the people looked unfriendly when we slowed down to inspect a
possible site. Finally, near Songerlu, we saw a village in the
distance on a hillside. We turned off the road that led to it, and
parked in a dry stream bed which looked promising. But before
we got very far in unloading the car, four farmers arrived and

investigated our arrangements. They gave us to understand that the mosquitoes were bad at our site, and one farmer motioned toward a nearby house where tractor-powered machinery was thrashing some crop. We should camp there, he indicated, and when we followed him, he led us to an empty field.

There we parked and started supper. Pretty soon the word got out, and more farmers started assembling, sitting in a large half-circle around us, watching every move of the preparation. Evening show! Good instinct of showmanship required to survive such an experience. The prosperous though quite unshaven farmer who had asked us there soon brought out an enormous plate of curds. Lloyd had no trouble with this unsolicited gift, but Sue, who can scarcely face even milk, turned a little pale. But everyone was watching — not a chance of disposing of it by any manner other than eating it.

When the daylight finally faded, the helpful farmers brought over the tractor, turned its lights full on us, and critically observed our bedtime oblations. Nothing like brushing your teeth with twenty men watching intently! Late show! We were pretty tired by this time, and most troubled about how we'd tell our audience that the show was over. We made up the bed, drew the curtains, came over to face our audience directly, bowed in unison and said good night. The farmers murmured a friendly return greeting, lumbered to their feet and went away, avidly discussing the evening's events among themselves.

On to Samsun after morning show. The head farmer asked us to take a buddy of his to a nearby town, which we did. At Samsun, we explored the possibility of taking a ship through the Black Sea to Trabzon. We were told that for 37 lira we and the car could get to Trabzon, provided we stayed in the car instead of in a cabin.

The ship, they said, would leave the next morning at 6 a.m., and arrive at 4 p.m. We decided such a trip would be a pleasant change from the road, and agreed to return the next morning. That left us with a leisurely afternoon to waste.

While we were at the shipping office, we inquired after a restaurant and a friend of the manager, a gaunt, tall, hawk-nosed, good-looking fellow in white shirt and white flannel trousers offered to show us the way. His name, he told us, was Yusef. He took us down some doubtful alleys, ending up at a nice sea-side cafe with terrace overlooking the port. Here we ate a good meal, selected after Yusef and Lloyd both peered into several pots in the kitchen. We drank a good beer with the meal (Turkish Biero). The meal, like others in Turkey, consisted of liver or lamb in pieces in a sauce with peppers. For dessert we had two kinds of melon, one a watermelon, the other resembling a cantaloupe.

All our conversation with Yusef, who ate nothing himself but supervised the serving of our meal, was in pictures on pieces of paper. He was from Rize, another town on the Black Sea, and visiting at Samsun. When the bill came, he took it and paid, ignoring our vigorous protests. Next he took us to a bathing beach, where we had a wonderful swim in the Black Sea. Sue was extremely conspicuous, the only woman swimming, and in a bathing suit at that. It was very awkward for the men who were all in the habit of changing on the beach. There was a lot of staring.

We returned to town, took our leave of Yusef, and wound our way up one of the mountains overlooking the port. We had thought that it would be pleasant to camp with a view to the sea, but we soon were uneasy about the campsite. First a man with a shotgun passed us. Next came a man with goats. Then a man with a pistol in his belt stopped to talk to us. Next came a man with more goats. We went to bed with a queasy feeling. Why all the guns? we wondered. We started up from a troubled sleep an hour later to a banging noise on the car tires. We listened a moment, and the banging returned, alternating with the sound of a clear, short whistle. We looked at one another in the dark, sitting there in our defenseless little pajamas. Lloyd picked up the flashlight, softly parted the curtain, flashed on the beam and summoned up his best courageous-voice-to-frighten-off-criminals. The criminal, a poor little shepherd with some fifty sheep, was squatting on the ground investigating our car and whistling to his sheep around it. Lloyd's peremptory voice stopped him for a moment, and then, whether to give himself courage or because he was unimpressed by us, he began to chant softly, and gradually moved away.

Arrived at shipping co. at 6:30 only to discover that information we had received the preceding day was all wet. Instead of 10 hours, the trip would take 24—14 more than by road. We were outraged, cursed the fool who had spoken to us the day before, regretted the afternoon we could have spent driving. A western-looking Turk at the office was equally disappointed. He too had been misinformed. His French-speaking friend asked us to take him along to Trabzon. We liked his looks and agreed. Ozkan turned out to be a machine engineer who was installing heating and air-conditioning in Trabzon. He was a quiet-spoken, pleasant man who had some German, so we could communicate.

The trip from Samsun to Trabzon was magnificent. The view from the heights across green hazelnut groves and red tile roofs fell to the Black Sea. The winding road made difficult driving, giving us the choice of breaking our necks while passing the buses on the curvy road or choking in their dust. If any of the three of us got thirsty or had business behind a bush, the others would look out for buses behind. If one came, whatever was going on was interrupted and we would all jump and race off so as not to be passed.

A pleasant lunch in a restaurant in Ordu was enlivened by a red-headed Englishman from the Air Group and radar unit at Ordu who leaned his head in the street level window and chatted with us a while. NATO forces radar units have been established in a lot of towns along the Black Sea, presumably to keep an eye out for anything coming across from the north.

Sometime after Ordu we had tea in a little village. After chairs were brought and we were seated in the middle of the main street in front of the post office, tea was brought. Behind the tea arrived a beautiful Turkish girl with a blouse cut sufficiently low to cast doubts on her devotion to Koranic law. She introduced herself as Tomris Kademoglu. As she sat down on the chair which appeared as soon as she did, she stood out like the proverbial rose among the thorny crowd that had gathered. She had studied at the American College (for women), Istanbul (we are not sure of the correct name of the school), where her prosperous father, a hazelnut merchant, had sent her. We were asked to admire her yearbook ("Tomris' wit was enjoyed by all, and the stage would profit if she would become an actress"), studded with pictures of devoted, and determined looking English and American teaching-ladies. Her father normally lives in Istanbul, but he had come North for the hazelnut harvest. She was obviously bored by the small town life and regarded our visit a pleasant interlude. When she could not persuade us to stay some days, she elicited a promise to write. No charge for the tea. In mid-afternoon we broke off the trip, climbed into bathing suits and jumped into the ocean 100 yards from the road. We arrived in Trabzon after dark, and after some inquiries were directed to the headquarters of the US Military Group, about whom we had heard from the English at Ordu. The group's headquarters were in a large house behind the usual wall, at the top of a narrow, steeply pitched alley that led at almost a 45-degree angle a mile through closely set buildings and walls. Five or six men were lounging in T-shirts in a large room, next to a pantry where our furtive looks could catch glimpses of Campbell's tomato soup and corned beef hash. They appeared to be not at all surprised to see visitors from the States, but were cordial and immediately responded to our inquiries about a place to camp with a suggestion of the local radar installation at which they assist the Turkish Army.

We ate dinner in town at a very pleasant restaurant, where the waiter brought out a much fingered menu which some careful American had translated in pencil. Beer and some meat in a sauce, and cucumbers in yogurt. Yogurt is becoming more and more conspicuous — mixed with water it becomes a drink, with cucumbers a salad, and often it is eaten just by itself.

Speaking of food and drink: beer can be had at reasonable prices throughout Turkey, though Islam does not permit drinking. Water is brought to the table in special bottles, though this does not speak for the source — it is more a symbol than a guarantee of pure water. We drank it once or twice when there was no beer. The conditions under which food is prepared — one can usually look in the pot, except at very fancy establishments — are unappetizing, but we liked our food and didn't get sick.

The great asset of Turkey, and we sorely missed it in Iran, was the ever present well. Wherever there was a source of water along the road, a pipe had been put in a wall, usually with a basin underneath. The pipes signified a fresh spring. We drank from them throughout the land, unless a house seemed to be immediately above or some other possible source of contamination. We also used them for "air-conditioning" — i.e. whenever we came to one we splashed off our faces and arms and drove on dripping. Delicious!

For the rest, we consumed unending amounts of fruit, replenishing with peaches and tomatoes and grapes and plums once or twice a day. In Iran, we added watermelons and other melons to our list — one large, juicy, cantaloupe-style melon usually was all we required for lunch. On the road from Trabzon to Erzurum, where bright orange patches on the mountain-sides announced the places where apricots were being dried, we relieved many little girls of big plates of fresh-picked apricots at very little cost. As a result our digestion, which became the subject of major interest to us on the trip, was usually splendid.

Until half-way through Turkey, we used to have three major meals a day — i.e. a major meal is one for which the stove is used. But the midday heat in Turkey turned lunch to such a chore that we gave it up. From then into India we usually had dried fruit and nuts, which we stocked at the bazaars in Istanbul and Teheran, some fresh fruit, and tea prepared in the morning. For breakfast, we had hot coffee (Turkish, but without so much sugar and not so thick), bread and jam, and occasionally eggs, when Sue thought the bazaar merchant looked reliable. She only asked once when they had been laid: the merchant who knew a little English answered, "tomorrow."

Dinner we ate out sometimes if there was a fairly decent restaurant (our standards were an absence of abscessed children), but usually we camped in the country. There we ate up our supply of tin cans, purchased in Graz: Wein-Beuschel at Songerlu, Kaiserfleisch at Mt. Ararat, Selchwurst near Herat. The cans were replenished — at outrageous prices — at Teheran.

But back to Trabzon. We slept that night on top of a mountain at Trabzon, immediately outside the barbed wire of the radar, possibly missile, installation. The Americans requested the bayonet-armed Turk guards to keep an eye out for our safety. No shepherds that night.

August 6

Glorious drive from Trabzon to Erzurum, through mountains reminiscent of the Salzkammergut. Slow driving because of many curves. Apricot country. The dry lowlands were relieved by rows of tall poplars, obviously planted by someone anxious to add some greenery. Above Erzurum, at a number of small towns, we began to notice a proliferation of the army installations which were prominent throughout Turkey. All appeared in a high state of readiness: hundreds of trucks lined up in apple-pie order, jeeps, cannon, and all in great quantity. Before Erzurum itself we passed the climactic one of these establishments. We were just remarking to each other that for a determined spy the situation around Erzurum would be sheer duck-soup, when we were flagged down by an armed soldier. Our passport was demanded

42 and swiftly borne off toward one of a series of indistinct low buildings in the distance. While Lloyd cursed softly, we watched the passport re-emerge from its first destination and travel about to four different buildings in the middle distance. A half hour later a junior officer returned with it, and in his sparse German cheerfully indicated that he would now climb into our vehicle and accompany us elsewhere. Fifteen miles later we entered Erzurum, after several interludes during which our companion stopped us and kept the Turkish army running by sending men in all directions to dig up gasoline for a stranded, gasless jeep. (The gasoline transfer was accomplished via our tea funnel, which he spotted on the front shelf of our car.) Eventually our passports were left at the police station, after being registered in immense, painfully written record books at two guard houses on the way. We were told we might pick them up in the morning, and where, please, did we plan to spend the night? In the car! Well, then our companion would arrange to find a place to park the car.

The selected site turned out to be a rather bare garden behind a local police station. There we set up our table and chairs, and while the local inspector chased off urchins we prepared supper. Our meal, which we took five yards from the side entrance of the station, was enlivened by the spectacle of two ladies of doubtful and overdressed appearance who arrived in a horse-drawn carriage with candle-lit side-lantern. Their mission was to bring simple and more comfortable clothes to a third lady of obviously doubtful profession who was awaiting incarceration on the other side of the front steps. To Lloyd's great discomfiture, she accomplished her change of apparel in the shadows of the front steps. All three were fascinated by us, and inquired at length about our offences. As far as we could make out, the inspector told them that we were above their inquiries.

August 7

We spent a comfortable night to the occasional protesting sounds of new prisoners arriving. During breakfast we were able to observe the furtive movements of two or three pathetic types who were smuggling cigarettes and food to friends in the barred cellar cells within our view. Lloyd went out to get bread and a fresh bag of good Turkish coffee.

After breakfast we picked up our passports and a soldier who escorted us 40 miles beyond Erzurum, through extended training areas which Lloyd identified as engineering, artillery, armor, and transportation.

The reason for the large concentration of men and equipment in this area is plain on the map. Erzurum is the closest major city to the Russian border along the main overland route from Russia into Turkey. As far as we could see, the Turks have much more equipment than the Yugoslavs. Their soldiery is not nearly as spiffy in appearance as that of the Greeks, approximating that of the Yugoslavs. But we were impressed with their apparent preparation.

Overall impression of Turkey: these fierce looking little people are very hospitable, much more so than their unshaven faces would indicate, and incredibly curious. Toward the end of Turkey, the invariable peering began to get on our nerves. But we loved the country, and found it very beautiful.

Toward evening, as we neared Dogobayazid and the border, a mountain suddenly rose from the plain and into the clouds. Because the clouds on its crown dimmed the sun, it looked black and forbidding. We located it on the map; 5165 meters high Ararat-Bu Agri Dagi — Mount Ararat, where Noah's Ark landed. Because it is relatively isolated on an enormous plain — there are a few lesser mountains by it — it is immensely impressive. We could see it still long after we had driven into Persia.

The Turkish and Iranian border stations peacefully share a common compound — the buildings lie around a large court. Border formalities took no longer than usual — we always take books with us when we have any official business to transact. It's better for our tempers.

Just inside Iran, we arrived at the small town of Maku where we saw a hotel sign on the left. Reluctant to camp out in a country for which we had no feel as yet, we decided to try it. We drove through a gate in the high mud walls into a lush and unkept garden, where a grazing cow stood by a small brook, while a man was driving two calves toward some outbuildings. In the garden stood a large two-storied villa, whose decayed whitewash and paneless windows announced a ruined elegance.

Presently a woman with a large shawl drawn over her lower face came out. We communicated to her that we were interested in staying, but, in view of the uninviting condition of the house, that we wished to do so in the car. She nodded, and with kerosene lantern in hand led us off into the villa, presumably to register us. Night had fallen by this time and the kerosene lantern was the only light in the dark halls. We went up some steps, down a long hall, and began to mount a staircase. In one of the high ceilinged rooms at the head of the staircase we caught a glimpse of children on the floor on some mats — one had the impression that these people did not live in the house, they camped in it. Eventually we arrived at a locked door which our guide carefully opened with a large key. Triumphantly she lit the interior: a bedroom, with two iron bedsteads, one covered with a shiny red satin quilt, the other with a blue satin quilt.

After this resplendent revelation, we once more sought to communicate our intention of sleeping in the car. This time we succeeded. We were shown a stagnant pond in another part of the garden where it was suggested we might wash. (We didn't — we used brook water.) Later a fine looking old man brought us a stoppered pottery jar which, he said, contained su (Turkish for water. The Persian is ab — crucial words on such a trip) for drinking. Since we couldn't see the source, we boiled the water for tea. We did not enjoy our meal, because as we began, the children who lived in the outbuildings began to congregate around us — and not one of them was whole. They looked like a display for UNICEF: all had sores, several had at least one eye that was half-closed and buttering, one pretty little girl had a charcoal black area around her mouth and chin. Only the children of the woman who lived in the big house were whole. To make matters worse, two big dogs belonging to the establishment expectantly guarded our dinner table, interrupting only to chase away an interloping dog. We were very pleased that we had not taken the room — and decided that our insecurity in a new land should not drive us to such a habitation again. Eventually the children and various goats and sheep and calves streamed away into the small outbuildings, where we assumed they would all spend an uncomfortable night.

The proprietor eventually arrived also, a tall, good-looking, serious man. He brought us a gas lamp, and tried to persuade us to stay in the house, but we declined.

August 8

After a breakfast which failed to interest us because of the reappearance of our youthful observers, we brushed off the last fly and climbed into our car with relief. To crown this distasteful experience, our handsome host charged us 50 rials — about $.75, outrageous for what it was. About ten miles beyond Maku, still within view of Ararat, we saw a car with European plates in a field, and by it two blond young men in blue shorts and nothing else — a rare sight in this area where everyone covers himself.

We went off the road and drove over. Roger and Martin Berthou turned out to be Englishmen and brothers. Martin was on his way to take up a post as 3rd Secretary at the British Embassy in Teheran. Roger, who was studying language and literature at Cambridge, was along for the ride. They were cheerful and pleasant, and we compared experiences in Turkey — they had come the same road as we. We crossed paths three or four times more that day, sharing afternoon tea on a hillside and quarreling with the same local policemen. We agreed that if our arrivals in Teheran coincided, we would meet.

That day's driving was hot and dry and dull. In every medium-sized town we were stopped for our passport, but unlike in Turkey, the policemen drove away the assembling crowds. The Persians are considerably taller than the Turks, with more open faces and a more refined appearance. Toward evening we arrived in Tabriz, an unimposing town. Like other Persian cities of various sizes, it announces its emergence from the village class by one or more large traffic circles planted with purple, pink and white petunias. We camped several miles beyond Tabriz near the road, at an undistinguished spot in a depression downhill from the highway. Since we already knew the Brrrrs and Tch Tchs of the shepherds, we were not disturbed by the flocks that passed in the night.

August 9

A grueling day of dull driving. Hills and plains all equally dry. Our one amusement was the camels which we now began to encounter in large numbers. They are great, lumbering pompous things, who peer along their noses with an air of contempt while chewing with their big, soft, fuzzy lips. Their gait is loose and uncoordinated looking when they run, though they have a fine swaying and dipping rhythm when they walk. They are led by a rope attached to a pin in their noses, a necessary device since they are often ornery. They are still a very important means of transport in these parts, though more so East of Teheran than West of it.

We made one depressing discovery during the day. We had bought some rials (the official rate was 75 rials to the dollar, the unofficial 78 to the dollar) under peculiar conditions shortly before leaving Turkey. We inquired at the bank, and were told that the bank had no rials. We were then taken by a bank clerk to a gentleman named Ahmed Bay, who presided over a dark and dusty room behind a hardware store. He sold us rials at 40 to $1, peeling the rials off a fat mixed bundle of foreign currencies that lay in a corner of his desk. Since we had no idea of the exchange rate (not in the Chase National Bank booklet) we had to take it. Now we needed more money to get to Teheran, but it turned out that Friday is the Sunday of Islam, and all banks were closed. We asked advice from an Iranian who had studied chemistry at Temple, Mr. Afsar-Keshmiri. We met him because we and another Iranian with a dumb little round blonde of a German wife were traveling the same road as we in a Chrysler. He had no advice but lent us 50 rials, which just saw us through.

We hoped to get to Teheran that night, but the last 60 miles before the city turned out to be the worst we had yet encountered — dusty, holey, with washouts and dangerous places everywhere. Yet this road was the busiest we had seen in all of Persia, buzzing with the incredibly high, overloaded trucks which are the bane of its roads and which here and there lie toppled by their load into ditches — warnings that the trucking laws of the country may not be adequate, or are inadequately enforced. To stay behind these trucks on the road was death — because the diesel smoke and dust would blind and poison you. To pass was disaster, because if the black diesel smoke came from a left-hand exhaust all view was obscured, even of bright oncoming headlights; if you got through the smoke the chances were a washout on the left would catch you. After two hours struggling, in which we covered thirty miles, we gave up, pulled off the road into the desert which bore only a prickly, unkind weed on its dry face, and made camp in the dark. We ate more dried fruit, but we were so tired we had almost no appetite. Our ritual ablutions — washing the face and brushing the teeth keeps men human — comforted us and we instantly fell asleep.

August 10

A few more hours on the road in the morning, when we felt refreshed enough to face that ghastly road again, saw us in Teheran. We went to the Park Hotel, knowing that it was the most elaborate in the city, but feeling that we had deserved all the luxury Teheran could offer. We hadn't slept at a hotel since Istanbul.

Two days at the Park cost us approximately 2000 rials or around $26, including good meals. We didn't get their fanciest suite — the air-conditioned rooms in the new building were all occupied, and our bath was down the hall, the furniture was oldish and the decoration very poor. But to us it seemed like heaven — a large, high-ceilinged room, as many showers as one could want, lots of water, water, water. We must have sent the poor servant scurrying at least once an hour for a fresh pitcher of ice-water.

We had some trouble finding the Park. It hides its light under a bushel, or more precisely, behind a wall whose gate is guarded by a mustachioed, grey-haired, distinguished fellow who betrays that he is no retired British major only when he responds in Pharsee. We inaugurated our stay — we arrived at 10 a.m. — with a huge breakfast in our room, to compensate for the dinner and breakfast we hadn't eaten. Then we slept an hour, and ventured out to find the bank. We still had no Persian money. We found the bank at 12:05, only to be told by a friendly Armenian gentleman who translated for us that the bank closed at 12 noon. It would re-open at 5, but only to receive money, not to pay out.

We asked him where we could find the post office. He indicated that it was just a few steps, and insisted on taking us. On the way, we discovered that he had taught himself English, largely through movies and movie magazines. When we arrived at the post office half an hour and 10 degrees heat later, we found a postcard from Mother R., and gratefully returned home in a cab.

This cab, like all human, mechanical, and animal propelled cabs had no fixed rate. In fact, a great deal has no fixed rate, and this usually redounds to the benefit of the vendor. He does you a service; you know payment is required; if you ask the price, he shrugs his shoulders and indicates that you in your wisdom will no doubt pay him a just amount. If you in your wisdom guess too low, he will reject the money altogether, and you, properly intimidated, will raise the rate much too high. If, on the other hand, you guess too high, you will rarely receive an indication that you have done so — although one cab driver once gave Lloyd 10 rials back. The matter of tips, car and tonga fares and other financial transactions residing within the hazy and uncertain sphere of perpetually evolving custom gave us more psychic pains than any fears of foreign lands, delays of customs officials, dusty roads and hot deserts. The dissatisfied look of a servant — which might appear even when we had paid adequately — could depress us for hours, and set us to fruitless discussions in which, by the application of reason, we attempted to arrive at concepts of a "just price." Fruitless, because the amounts are not based on objective criteria like the value of services rendered, but rather on indefinable, only intuitively perceivable factors, like his status, your status, his persistence, your intimidatability, etc., etc. In any case, it is wise to have a lot of change, because giving a man

5 rials when you want 3 back already resolves the matter in his favor. He has no 3 rial change!

Back at the hotel we slept some more, waking up at 3 to venture out again into the baked and almost deserted streets. Around 1 p.m. Teheran goes to sleep, and it doesn't come back to full activity until almost 5. The metal or wooden roll-down shutters come down; only a few shops with sleepy attendants stay open, and one or two women in black shawls that cover the western clothes they wear beneath scurry back and forth in the heat of the day.

Finding almost no one on the streets whom we could ask for directions, we drove around the town, quietly perspiring under Rover's tropical roof, searching for the Land-Rover service. Eventually we found it, and made clear our wishes by means of the Land-Rover shop-manual and a little English. With the help of three mechanics, we unloaded the dusty camping equipment into a storage room and perspiring more heavily, withdrew by cab to our quiet room and shower at the Park Hotel. There, surrounded by Time magazines (which one learns to read because it is the main source of American news as one travels east) and The New York Times, we caught up on the flow of news, and noted that the Democratic convention would take place while we were in Afghanistan.

August 11

Today we put in a new supply or dried fruit and nuts. Since Sue was doubtful of the bazaar tins in which they were stored, and more doubtful of the hands that had dried them, she washed them all in the sink, and spread them out on newspapers all over the hotel room. The maid who came to turn down the beds appeared to find this unusual, but since our Pharsee was non-existent, we swept grandly out of the room and left her unenlightened.

We purchased a new tin water container and several more screw-top jars to hold supplies. Since we had run out of European raspberry jam, the confinement of Turkish and Persian jams, which are practically fluid, had become an insuperable problem. No matter what we put the gooey stuff in, it ran all over the supply box during a day's drive. The absolutely foolproof screw-top metal jar we bought that day made us overconfident, with the result that we had to de-goo everything after the first day's drive from Teheran. Even so, we refused to part with our jam, because after Yugoslavia we bought no butter (couldn't keep it) nor eggs (too doubtful), and the jam was crucial for an edible breakfast.

The visit to the National Bank was enlightening. Since Iranian currency is realistically valued (at official rate it is 75 rial to the dollar, and the black market 78), we were quite content to cash money officially. But we also wanted some Afghan and Pakistan money, in case it should happen to be Friday when we arrived in either of those places. Pakistan money they had — at a rate of 4 rupees to $1.00. The official Pakistan rate is Rs 4½ or almost 5 to the dollar, and 6 on the black market, but we didn't know that and lost accordingly. Afghanis they had none, but the free market, the bank official told us, would have some. Where might the free market be found, we inquired. "There" he said, pointing to a long row of ordinary waiting benches running up the middle of the long floor of the bank. And indeed, seated on these benches and standing near, were perhaps a hundred reputable and disreputable looking men, some of them murmuring as they counted little pink stacks of rial notes before them, others carrying on loud discussions with one another. The bank official signaled to one of the more reputable looking, a squat, well-shaven man in a light blue suit carrying a briefcase. To him we communicated our interest in Afghanis. (The name of the unit of money; the national is referred to as an Afghan, with a throaty "ch" or expectorating sound on the "gh.") He in turn conferred with two or three less respectable looking types, and returned with an offer, which we suddenly realized we had no way of judging, since we had seen no exchange rates on Afghanis quoted. So we excused ourselves from the free market and trotted to the British Embassy which was near the bank, and where we thought someone would advise us.

There we discovered that the Berthous had come in the night before, and were now staying in a nearby flat nursing "the" disease. We also found that the new first (?) secretary of the Teheran Embassy, Hugh Carless, had just arrived from a vacation in Afghanistan, in a duplicate of our own vehicle. We spoke to him on the phone from the gate-house, and he suggested that he would join us at the Park that evening for drinks and to give us advice. He also advised us that Afghanis came at a better price in the Bazaar at Meshed than in Teheran.

At 6:30 we met with Carless, and the Berthous, whom we
had briefly seen in the morning. Carless avowed that Afghanistan
was quite feasible. Laughing, we told him of a horror story Lloyd
had heard from a warrant officer who had served at the Embassy
in Kabul. The story concerned a diplomatic car held up by bandits
on the road from Kabul to Peshawar. The car had been robbed
and diplomatic files scattered over the Afghan hills. We added
that we realized that his was just another one of those popular
horror stories people like to tell prospective travelers. Carless
laughed agreeably at that and added conversationally — "Yes,
I was in that car."

When we had recovered, he related the following tale: it
seems that a disaffected tribe had contrived an ambush on this
road, which goes in part through steep canyons and is quite
vulnerable to attack. Carless' car had been the first stopped, and
its occupants were put in a nearby canyon and guarded, while
for the next three hours other cars and lorries were held up in
the same ambush. One lorry was accompanied by two soldiers,
seated on top. One soldier, either through extreme courage or
extreme stupidity, fired his gun. He was instantly shot. The
other soldier sought to jump down to surrender, but his motives
were misunderstood, and he too was shot.

At darkness the ambush was lifted, and the bandits disappeared. When Carless finished his somber tale, he assured us
that such events were rare. He was the former secretary at the
Kabul Embassy and should know!

Departure from Teheran, with a suitcase full of clean laundry, a clean, dusted car and clean camping equipment. We had no idea when we started our trip how dirty the car would get on these roads. Every evening after we entered Persia, we had to spend an hour washing out the car before we could sleep in it. The dust of the road penetrated everywhere — into our food, our suitcases, our books. To depart from a city clean and pure, as we did from Teheran, was a splendid sensation. Rover had received as good service in Teheran as he had in Istanbul (except for the fact that a mechanic had failed to tighten the wheel bolts after switching around the tires, and Lloyd discovered the omission only after the car started to sway), and we were once more underway, for the hardest part of the journey.

Again those rolling, arid hills, relieved by small towns and by caravanserais. This relic of the day when only camel caravans traveled the road to the east is still a lively institution. A caravanserai may be more or less elaborate. Some have a small teahouse and three or four low bedsteads standing before the door. The bedsteads are usually simple wooden platforms with a Persian rug on top. The caravanserai has now become a stopping and refreshing place not just for the traditional caravan, but for the brightly painted buses that tool back and forth across Persia, their GM bodies and Cadillac tail fins gleaming. The caravanserai may be developing toward the ideal which Howard

Johnson — so despised by us while we were in the States, so longingly remembered now — represents on the turnpikes. Some have a pool of fresh or fetid water, some stands where melon and grape merchants hawk their wares, bedsteads placed under trees around the pool to keep cool, and — oh sweet memory of restrooms at Amoco stations — several bomb-site Johns.

Since we are a nation in which toilet habits receive a good deal of anxious attention, a word about conditions on such a trip. The deserts are wide and lonely between Persia and Pakistan, and Yugoslavia and Turkey are rich in bushes. Only in India and Pakistan, where there are few empty spaces and every bush has a bullock and its owner behind it, do natural processes become a problem for him or her who requires privacy.

We spent the night at Sharud, at a quiet little caravanserai by a clean, fast-running stream. The owner, who had no other business, was our guest for a cup of tea and a biscuit. The three or four modern young men of Sharud — recognizable by their clean, starched, white shirts and slacks — came and stood by and amiably tried their little English on us.

Those that count in this part of the world can normally be distinguished by a simple sign — they are freshly shaven. Those that don't count or count a little don't grow full-fledged beards. They just neglect to shave for a week or so at a time. The sign is obviously not reliable — how can you tell if the shaven man before you isn't a no-account whom you have caught on his day of shave? But it's a reasonable indication.

On to Meshed, after an unsuccessful attempt to pay the keeper at the caravanserai of the night before. We stopped at Subzawar to take a picture of a funny mosque with aluminum topped minarets. The crowd that gathered to watch us was rude, and the children very fresh. We drove off quite angry. In the medium-sized cities after Teheran where we stopped for fruit and benzin this was often the case. A batch of just pre-puberty males would gather around, stick their heads in the window unless Lloyd growled, and make remarks which sounded no less fresh for being in Pharsee. We had the feeling, although we had no evidence, that the extraordinary sight of an unveiled, barelegged woman led them to suppose that such an immoral phenomenon invited disrespect. The women became increasingly more veiled as we moved east — the large black or dark blue cotton shawl, worn as a cloak over the ordinary western style clothes which all the city and many provincial women wear, is rarely drawn over the face in Teheran, where women even use lipstick while wearing it. But east-ward, the face is more rarely seen, and the casual gesture of hiding the face becomes more purposeful, until finally women squat down, turn away and draw the veil when a car passes. In Teheran women are fairly casual about what they wear on that part of the leg which shows below the shawl, but by Meshed, black or dark brown stockings, hot and uncomfort-able looking, hide all offending outline and flesh. By the time we arrived in Meshed, Sue was feeling self-conscious about her face showing — if people look at it as though it were naked, then gradually the supposition rises that it is naked.

Relations among men from Turkey on seemed much warmer than in the west. There is a great deal of unselfconscious display of physical tenderness between them — holding hands and embracing are common. Perhaps the fact that women are not usually companions here, but keepers of the home and bearers of children who have no knowledge of the outside world makes companionship of men more intense.

In Meshed we looked for the Bhakta Hotel which is run by an Armenian and was recommended by Carless. The Bhakta, which is not prepossessing, was full and the proprietor sent us to a subsidiary, the Hotel Meamee. (Only the morning light on the flaking sign told us that this was in fact the Hotel Miami — the name should not lead anyone to suppose that Miami Beach standards are being approximated.) The establishment turned out to be rather depressing, though clean sheets were spread after Lloyd made a nose while examining those on the beds when we arrived. Our stay was enlivened by frequent visits of the tiny, uncouth, busybody of a manager, who crashed into our room twice without knocking and rushed upstairs from time to time to check if we had turned off the light in the john and the water at the hall tap. He gave Sue a dressing-down when she left the latter running while going to fetch her soap.

We had decided to report to the Consul at Meshed before leaving for Afghanistan, and tried to find him that evening since we hoped to leave early in the morning. The Consul, Robert

Shott, was entertaining an Iranian general, but came out to get our names. When we told him we were looking for Afghanis, he suggested we meet him in the morning. He and one of the consulate servants would take us to the bazaar.

While we were looking for the way to the consulate, four young Iranians accosted us and offered their help. Two of them, it turned out, were taking English lessons several nights a week, and were very anxious to practice it. They were perhaps seventeen or eighteen, and eager to hear about America and western habits in general. The brighter one of the two was the son of a Persian rug merchant, and gave us as a parting gift his English translation of some stories concerning a Persian comic folk figure, a Till Eulenspiegel type called Mollah. The other, an engineering student, told us that Mossadeq was very popular still, though he had little chance for a comeback because he would not be permitted to hold public office. They invited us for tea and apple juice at a little ice cream parlor, and escorted us safely back to the hotel. Just as well — the consulate, which is big and lovely, is located off a narrow back alley which is reached by more devious alleys — not the sort of place one wants to walk alone at night.

August 14

After some minor rigmarole about our passports — they didn't come back on time — we met Shott at the consulate. He showed us around the consulate: it has elaborate, high rooms, with rich painted plaster floral wreathing on some ceilings, and was still hung with rather good Chinese hanging and modern paintings belonging to Shott's predecessor, Cassily. While we were with him, Shott had occasional aside conferences with a servant who was engaging plumbers and such to improve the sanitary arrangements to the level of the rest of the buildings. The compound, which lies behind simple walls, has three courtyards overgrown with flowers: one for the servants, one intended for the seraglio of the rich Persian builder of the house, and one for the men. Since Shott as well as his associates appear to be happy monogamists, the latter two courts have lost their special purpose. One has a very small swimming pool, and both are used for pleasant garden sitting.

Shott and one of the Iranian Embassy employees accompanied us to the Meshed bazaar, which stretches along a long, narrow street whose buildings shut out the sun and leave the shops on both sides in murky shadows. It was the first bazaar, the first street in the east for that matter, in which we both felt distinctly foreign, if not unwanted, and for good reason. The Iranian consulate personnel had been nervous about the whole expedition, and especially about Sue's accompanying the men into the bazaar. The day of our trip preceded by only one day the great and sorrowful feast day of the Shiite Moslems commemorating the death of Hussein, a descendant of the Prophet and, according to the Shias, his true heir. Meshed, with its great shrine containing the tomb of Imam Riza, is a famous pilgrimage center for the Shias, and the death-day of Hussein is the culmination of months of sorrowing, comparable in a sense to our Lent and Good Friday. Foreigners are not welcome at these tunes of great religious significance.

We went to the bazaar with some trepidations, after Sue had modified her wanton appearance with a scarf over her head. Because of the impending feast, all money changers in the bazaar were closed. We were about to give up, when our Iranian consulate guide came back from some inquiries and announced: "One Jew is open." Apparently the ancient profession is still practiced in these parts by the people of the Book, and they are not bound by the Moslem festivities. The money changer quoted us an acceptable rate, and then went off to see if he could round up enough Afghanis to cover the deal. He told us the transaction would take another 20 minutes. By this time a crowd was beginning to gather, and while the men seemed mostly curious and not unfriendly, an inordinate number of little boys were accidentally taking running starts and bumping into Sue, without being chased off by the adults. Shott suggested we leave the consulate servant there to finish the transaction and start back to the consulate. Half-way through the bazaar we heard chanting ahead, and caught some glimpses of black prayer flags. Shott hastily shepherded us into a nearby bake shop, and only just in time. The chanting signaled the approach of a mourning procession, on its way to a shrine in the bazaar. Men bearing black prayer flags came first, followed by a slow-moving array of mourners — men with shaven heads, wearing loose black sleeveless gowns that were cut out to expose the shoulder blades. They carried short clubs to whose heads were attached some

twenty thin metal chains, and with these they beat their exposed
backs rhythmically as they walked — the self-flagellation was
not violent, but steady and ritually patterned.

As they passed we huddled toward the rear of the bake shop
and watched the bakers at work. They squatted on a brick floor,
and accomplished their work with a primitive division of labor.
The dough was mixed in a back room where we couldn't see it, but
then it was brought out. The first man shaped it into equal sized
round balls, which he threw to the second, who dexterously drew
it into a flat, inch-thick three cornered sheet with his hands,
and then, moistening his fingers, punched a pattern all along its
length. A third man laid the sheet on a kind of large, hard pillow,
and lowered it into a hole in the floor which turned out to be the
oven. The unleavened sheets came out brown some time later, and
were handed to a little boy who hung them on two nails on the
wall. It was our experience that these loaves are quite tasty when
warm and fresh, but they don't keep fresh very well. We usually
tried to get them fresh for another reason — they are displayed
in large piles on stands by the dusty roads (in rural areas), and
the fresher they are the less risk you take.

When the procession had passed, we returned to the consulate, where we undertook another expedition — for fresh water.
This was available at the American Missionary Compound, a
series of pleasant, peaceful buildings behind a high wall. There we
met Mrs. Cochrane, dean of the foreign colony of Meshed. She
is a big, grey-haired woman, wife of the doctor who heads the
mission hospital. She speaks Persian, apparently fluently, and

keeps what in those circumstances struck us as a really splendid household — she cans peaches, serves home-baked cookies,
keeps a house which, though none of the furniture or art was in
outstanding taste, gives an impression of graciousness, with its
ferns on the porch and flowers inside.

Mrs. Shott and Mrs. Cochrane discussed the missionary
picnic, which was planned for the following night — a plan which
the consul clearly considered hare-brained since the time coincided precisely with the great festivities. Mrs. Shott quoted
the Persians at the consulate against the plan, Mrs. Cochrane
discussed the matter in Persian with her servants and came up
with contrary advice. We never found out how the thing came
out.

We left Meshed around 1 p.m., after equipping ourselves
with tire patches. We were guided to the road to Herat by a boy
from the local Land-Rover agent — he went with us for twenty
miles. The road toward the Afghan border passed through
Turbat-i-Shaik-Jam, the Persian border town. There we had
a conversation with Colonel Ansari, a smart looking officer with
a swagger stick who commanded the Persian border battalion.
Night fell as we passed through the No Man's Land between
the frontiers, past the Persian border guards with their fixed
bayonets gleaming in the early moon. After half an hour's driving, a border barrier loomed out of the darkness, and on the
right rose the shadow of an old fort. We sounded our horn,
waited. Nothing happened. We beeped again, and wondered if

we should camp here, by this barrier, or if we should risk lifting it and going on. Just then we heard the sound of running feet, and two figures emerged, from the darkness in the direction of the fort. The border guards. They cheerfully pumped Lloyd's hand in greeting, glanced at our passports, and indicated that one of them would now climb in to take us to some unknown destination ahead.

Another 15 minutes' driving brought us to a cluster of large mud buildings. Our companion directed us to the first of these, and as our headlights swung around they illumined the bobbing figures of two turbaned men near a distant wall — they were finishing the evening prayers on their knees, facing toward the direction whence we had come, towards Mecca.

At the top of the front steps of this building hung a kerosene lantern, illuminating the figures of eight or ten men who were presently joined by the two worshippers. The tallest of these, a young giant with a gentle face, wearing loose pajamas, a long shirt, and an embroidered cap, rose and heartily shook Lloyd's hand, then Sue's, greeting us with the "Salaam" which is the simple greeting in these parts. (The more elaborate is Salaam Aleichem — very near the Hebrew greeting.) Another man, in striped trousers and shirt but without any headdress, rose to greet us next. He was the border official. After him all the others, older bearded men with large, loosely wrapped turbans, rose and greeted us. Though Afghanistan imposes a stricter purdah on its women than any other Moslem country we passed through, the men were relaxed in their greetings to Sue. Since she was plainly not of a category with their women, they apparently treated her in the only other plausible way — as a man.

After chairs were brought for both of us, the passport officer began the examination of the passports while all the others sat around, and watched, or chatted with each other. Eventually another tall young man arrived in white trousers and shirt and short cropped hair. He leapt up the steps in huge, gangly strides, and greeted us gaily and with great warmth. He, we were informed, was the proprietor of the border hotel, and if we wished accommodations or meals, he would gladly provide both. We said we did want a meal and might want to sleep there, though we might sleep in the car — keeping the door open in case we didn't like it.

We drove the car over to the Hotel, which lay across a road and a courtyard from the customs building. It was a large brick structure, entirely unlit except for our host's kerosene lamp. He led us up the broad steps, past two more turbaned old men who continued their agile evening prayers (Moslem praying appears to require quite a lot of athletic prowess, involving extended and repeated bowing while on the knees) undisturbed by our passing down a long hall off which lay the rooms of the hotel — all empty — to the last room on the right. This he entered. The lantern which he placed on a small table revealed a large room with high ceilings and high windows, freshly white washed walls, a maroon Persian rug on the floor, three large iron bedsteads with good-looking brown and blue woolen blankets, and curtains of a handsome brown wool tweed at the doors. This, he indicated, was his first class room. He pulled two chairs up to the small table, asked us to be seated, and suggested a menu of eggs, bread, melon, grapes and tea. His English vocabulary extended to the eggs and grapes, our Persian to tea (chaay) and melon (charbuze — the spellings are phonetic). When we asked him if he spoke English, he looked deprecating: "Kam Kam English." This phrase we heard again and again in Afghanistan. What the precise meaning is we don't know, but the significance was obviously "not so good."

About all this fresh fruit we ate at restaurants — we had no way of controlling if it was washed, or if so, in what water. Prudence dictates that we should not have eaten it, and in Afghanistan we certainly never drank any water we were served — always chaay. But we had fools' luck. Nothing happened.

The meal was pleasant, and since a brief examination showed the sheets were fresh though unironed, and the beds free of wild-life, we stayed.

August 15

The next morning we ate a similar breakfast, enlivened by our own Teheran cherry marmalade, and got underway. The mileage markers which had guided us through Persia now disappeared. They had served their function: teaching us Persian numerals, which we had to know for the financial transactions in Persia — we usually bargained by having a vendor write the amount on the dusty surface of our car door, and then writing the bargaining figure underneath.

The land from the border to Herat did not differ greatly from the last part of Persia. One difference was the road, which immediately announced that in Afghanistan we should not expect to travel more than 20 mph, and that the bouncing we had gotten on some Persian roads was insignificant. Another difference was a powerful hot wind which began to blow when we were not far into Afghanistan. It whipped up the dust and sand from the arid land and chased it over the road. When we stopped, as we had to four times that morning, to readjust and eventually completely reload the equipment in the back, it blew so strongly that we had trouble moving about. Once it tore the wooden folding table from Sue's hands. This is the "wind of 120 days" for which the area is famous — or infamous. Its unhesitating persistence tires the body and irritates the spirit. We were almost spitting at one another after an hour of it. The terrible, uneven road where even 15 mph was no guarantee against bounces that would send us flying out of our own seats, produced several disasters. The new aluminum water container, bought in Teheran, was crushed to an octagonal shape, and eventually the metal side gave way and the back of the car was flooded. We had six large book packages, wrapped in heavy paper, lying under the middle seat where the water could reach them. So 20 miles out of Herat we had to stop, rush around to save the packages and mop up the back. But it wasn't too bad. The wind had its virtues: it dried the book packages off quickly. Subsequently we discovered that only one book had been hurt, but that unfortunately was Lloyd's thesis (the binding).

We arrived at Herat around 12:30. It is a charming town. We saw its smokestacks — what industry could Herat have that requires four smokestacks? — rising in the distance some time before we reached the approach avenues which, though still uneven and graveled, are lined with beautiful coniferous trees of a kind we had not met before. The weary traveler from the country-side must find these a great relief as he goes to the city market to sell his goods. We certainly did. As we entered the city, we discovered that the smokestacks were broken-off minarets, the remains of an ancient University that dominated the East when Herat was a great center of culture and learning in the 16th century.

Susanne sitting near a tree.

Herat shows signs of more self-consciousness about its looks than many of the greater cities of the East that we passed through. The trees that impressed us as we entered line many of the major thoroughfares. Blue and white and lilac petunias as well as other plants survive in the hot sun in public places, and every major crossing is decorated with a policeman in sky-blue corduroy! The Herat municipality is responsible for this innovation, and we saw no imitators elsewhere. We passed through a lot of blue arches, and saw new or recently new buildings painted in a number of gay pastel shades, among which the same handsome blue predominates.

Everywhere frantic decorating was in progress in preparation for the Jeshed, or Independence Day Celebration which would begin August 24 and last a week. It celebrates the successful end of the last Afghan war, which finished British influence in Afghanistan. The man who won this independence for the Afghans, the former King Amanullah, was apparently cut of the same cloth as Ataturk. He sought to modernize his country and among other things to take the women out of Purdah. On this ground, among others, he incurred the wrath of the conservative elements, especially the mullahs, and was ousted. He is still living, reputedly in some European country. But this explanation of his fall is not only too brief but also too rational to be a true account of any incident in Afghan history. It is a land in which tribal and family rivalries are still significant, and they must have been more so in Amanullah's day. Quite possibly the westernizing dispute was compounded by such rivalries. It is also rumored that the British, mindful of their defeat at Amanullah's hands and possibly seeking a renewal of their influence, had a hand in his fall.

We heard more talk of history and politics in Afghanistan than in any other land en route, both from Afghans and foreigners. We knew little more of the country than that it had traditionally been the invasion (and trade) route to India; that therefore the British and Russians had spent a substantial part of the nineteenth century meddling in Afghan politics trying to create a situation favorable to themselves; that Afghanistan, though drawn into the British sphere of influence as far as its foreign policy was concerned, had resisted any real colonization and that the old game of seeking influence was not over, but had gotten some new players — notably the US. Since we knew little — and in fact not much is available — we were fascinated by all we heard and saw, and took more notes than elsewhere.

Afghanistan was plainly the wildest country we visited. Dean Mason's observations about social capital (especially communications and transportation) as a prerequisite for development struck us as never more apt than here. Afghanistan has no rail road whatsoever. The roads are such that only people with a covered wagon mentality would dream of crossing the land. This means that if heavy equipment (which cannot be flown in) is required anywhere, it must be brought in under incredible road conditions. Until a basic road or railway system is established, Afghanistan can hope for no light or heavy industry, we would judge. The factory might be built, but how would its products be distributed? It is something of a mystery to us how the Helmand Valley Project — a dam project built by a US firm under contract to the Afghan government — managed to get its materials in.

There is a telephone network — we know it well. The two wires accompanied us from Herat to Kabul. The Afghans also have an air service. We were told that the airport at Kabul is closed in the winter months, but though KLM will not land at that time, Air India will.

The attractively produced Afghan brochure which we received from the first secretary at the London Embassy assured us that "the new road building program is reaching completion." We quoted this to each other for the almost 1000 miles of road that we traveled from Herat to Kabul whenever some incredible stretch dimmed our spirits. But in Kabul, which was paved with Russian financial aid, we were told that a road system was planned toward the north — also with Russian aid. This development does not bring cheer to American hearts in Kabul. It is said that all the plans are for north–south roads, i.e. fine roads leading from Uzbekistan to Kabul. There is gloomy suspicion about that these roads are not meant only for trade; why no east–west roads?

One stretch of road, for 60 miles between Girisk and Kandahar, is a good, graded though gravel road. The US is said to have had a hand in it. But otherwise, the new road building program was nowhere in evidence.

The absence of even a rudimentary communications system, as well as of other evidence of western impact, led us to speculate on the virtues and vices of colonialism. The Afghans, alone of all the people we met in the Middle East and South Asia, were totally unapologetic about their lack of knowledge of western manners and ways. (Kabul may be an exception.) Elsewhere we had found people apologizing if they couldn't speak English. Here there was some surprise that we couldn't speak Pharsee or Pushtoo. An Indian acquaintance who spent time in jail as a nationalist has told us that he is often unintentionally resentful of westerners because "I forget that we are free." The Afghans have no such colonial memory, and none of the inferiority feelings associated with such a memory. If they are hostile to a westerner, they are hostile because westerners are infidels with doubtful customs and ways of life, not because the recollection of dominion makes westerners both admirable and hateful. The Afghan does not (yet) suffer from the love–hate conflict that seems to bother the peoples of former colonial areas in their relations with the west. His pride is undamaged.

This outlook has its negative side. It means that the Afghans in general have not yet acquired an awareness of modern technological possibilities (obviously there are many Afghans who are exceptions to this rule) or of the experiences of the west. The result is that Afghanistan presents an example of 16th and 17th century style oriental autocracy caught up in 20th century power political problems. Like the autocracies of an earlier era, Afghan politics are family politics uninformed by any regular-

74 ized determination of popular will — though elaborate claims of constitutional monarchy are made. As a result, the ebb and flow of prime ministers, even of the royal crown, are matters of palace intrigue rather than of electoral decision. Like the older autocracies, the Afghan government lacks the technological means to control its domain effectively — disaffected tribes that flaunt the central government's law and order have been a problem in the recent past. The government today is in the hands of the family of Zahir Shah, the present king. Until some years ago, one branch of the family was in control, during the premiership of Shah Mahmud. (His son, Zalmei Mahmud, was in Lloyd's class at Harvard. He never returned to Afghanistan, but is said to be writing his PhD in Geneva. Many are the reasons for PhD procrastination!) Shah Mahmud was on good terms with the Americans and other westerners, but we were told that his regime — though not necessarily he — was slow and corrupt. He was ousted and succeeded by another member of this complex family, a man named Daood. Unlike Shah Mahmud, Daood is relatively inaccessible, especially to the Americans. His regime has pursued closer relations with the Russians, probably because the Russians have been prepared to do more for Afghan development, and that is his overwhelming interest. US contributions to Afghan development have been relatively more meager (we have given about $40 million in loans) while the Russians have been very generous (they gave the Afghans about $105 million in low interest loans). Shortly before we arrived in Kabul Daood had slipped in his bath and taken a bad fall. There was

some sentiment in the western community that a more decisive accident would have been preferable.

The atmosphere in Kabul breathes intrigue, largely because speech, communications and political decision making must flow through subterranean channels — they are by no means free and open. The westerners to whom we spoke in Kabul almost to a man referred to Afghanistan as a police state (and some Indians whom we have met recently, who have been in Afghanistan with sports missions, seem to agree). To us the term seemed a misnomer — it conjures up visions of highly rationalized, bureaucratized, technologized western style dictatorship. From all we heard, the system sounded closer to the classical model of oriental tyranny. What exists in Afghanistan seemed to us more an ancient arrangement which had never heard of the liberal tradition, and didn't want to hear of it, than a modern arrangement seeking to suppress it.

As far as the symptoms were concerned, the westerners in Kabul chafe under them, and not unreasonably so. It is standard for all countries to maintain spies in foreign embassies, but the practice seems to have carried to a fine point here. We were told that not only did all the Afghans in the foreign embassies in Kabul have to report to the investigative services, but if any of them failed to report something a fellow employee had reported, he would be subject to a heavy penalty. The employees had responded as one might expect: they held a conference at the end of the day to pool information and decide on their common story.

Social intercourse among westerners and Afghans was stringently controlled. A Kabulian official, whom we met on the way to Kabul and who was quite cordial to us, regretfully told us that he could not invite us to his house. "It would not be understood." In another ten years, he thought, things might loosen up. We heard that invitees to western homes in Kabul had to receive official permission.

The Afghan newspapers, we were told, have to clear all their material with the ministries, and tend to restrict themselves to handouts. They are extremely touchy about foreign coverage — apparently both Time and Life had at one time run articles that were resented in these parts. The sharpest reaction was to an article — perhaps in Life, but we are not sure — referring to the King's "dancing girls." "Everybody knows the King has Mistresses," one veteran of Kabul told us, "but dancing girls! That implies frivolity!" They are also very sensitive about any pictures of Afghans in rags.

Shortly after we left Kabul, Abe Rosenthal, the N.Y. Times correspondent in India, was banned from Afghanistan, possibly because of some pretty competent articles written by a freelance couple.

The Pashtoonistan issue, which always seems somewhat esoteric when the Christian Science Monitor writes it up, is top news and politics here. One western writer was called in the government to explain an offensive article he had written: "You have referred to Pakistan as Afghanistan's neighbor!" the responsible minister said sternly. "Pakistan is not our neighbor.

The neighboring country is Pashtoonistan!" the writer, who was 77
fed up being called in to the ministry and also by the entire
Pashtoonistan squabble, retorted, "I want to go to this country
Pashtoonistan. Would you be so kind as to direct me to their
Embassy so I can get a visa?"

The brochure on Afghanistan which we received in London
has a map which shows Pashtoonistan as a separate country cut
out of portions of Pakistan. The US has apparently taken its
stand, on an agreement signed many years ago by an Afghan
King endorsing the present boundaries. Several Afghans
remarked, bitterly, "You always take a legal stand, when it suits
you and your friends."

We made no effort to explore the Pashtoonistan matter at length. It is as vexing as many other cases where self-
determination is called upon to decide a matter of nationality.
It is certainly quite possible that if only the Pushtoo speaking
peoples of Pakistan were asked to choose between Pakistan and
Afghanistan, they would opt for the latter. But why must the
issue be raised? By the same logic, why should not the Persian
speaking peoples of western Afghanistan be asked to choose
between Persia and Afghanistan? Probably the most solid
ground for such a question being asked at all is if the Pushtoos
are being in some sense discriminated against in their rights as
citizens of Pakistan. If they are, the additional question arises,
whether they should not be given a choice between Pakistan,
Afghanistan and total independence. At present, the Afghans
in their claim for the territory are having a lonely row, since their

demand has no threat of force behind it, and world opinion has by no means been mobilized on behalf of its claims. However, if she should get the support of Russia in the demand, together with command of the arms with which Russia is now beginning to supply her, she may be able to make the demand effective — or give it great nuisance value at the very least. Both India and Russia, though for different reasons, are not beyond backing the Afghans against Pakistani claim to the region.

Anyhow, there we were, driving into Herat at noon, watching the city being decorated for Independence Day. After some driving down wide streets and some agitated sign language with the nice sky-blue police, we arrived at the Park Hotel, a surprisingly large, well-kept establishment, with a western style entrance lounge. We were conducted to a rather ordinary dining room, Persian rug on floor, table-cloth of doubtful cleanliness, napkins ditto. We drank no restaurant water in Afghanistan, only hot chaay (tea). While we were eating, we met Ahmid Mullah, whom we had been told to expect there by Carless in Teheran. Ahmid Mullah in some respects reminded us of Fred Holborn, omni-informed, omnicurious, omnicompetent, and something of a lone wolf. A man of perhaps 35, he wore a white shirt, narrow black trousers, and a brown wool Karikul cap which sharpened his narrow intelligent face. He was quite reserved at first, but loosened up after a time. He speaks English, admires Lincoln and Washington (and possibly Roosevelt now — we gave him a long lecture on the subject), and is book hungry. He asked Carless for a long list of medical and chemical texts.

He conducted us through the mazes that must be traversed before one can buy gasoline in this country. All the gas comes from Russia in trucks — the first time we saw one we puzzled and puzzled trying to place the writing, which was obviously not Persian script. It is scarce and rationed. We understand there is a thriving and expensive black market, but if you get stamps you may buy at the fixed price which is fairly reasonable (about $.40 a gallon). The problem is getting the stamps. The way to procure them, to judge by our experience in Herat, is to go to no one less than the Provincial Director for Rationing himself. We arrived shortly after lunch, and found only lesser bureaucrats. One can make a rule (not an invariable one, but still a rule) that anyone who is wearing a turban in Afghanistan is not an important official. The corollary proposition does not hold. Not everyone who wears a fur hat is an important man. You have to know something about fur hats: some are fancier than others. The Director, when he finally showed up, had a very beautiful silver-grey one with long, flat curls of fur. So long as we were dealing with lesser officials via Ahmid Mullah, we could only get stamps for one tank in Herat. The next tank, we were told, would require further submissions to the office at Farah. Lloyd's gesticulation failed to move them. It was against the regulations, it was never done, it was not possible to get stamps to see us through Afghanistan. We have heard similar messages since we arrived in Pakistan and India, and have learned to rely on our built-in advantage as Sahib-types to always see the top man first. That goes for banks — we talk only to managers;

for post offices — we talk only to postmasters; and for other offices. After one becomes known at the institution, this is often no longer necessary, because the lower level types know that you have received official sanction. They are then no longer afraid to do things for you.

In this case, when the Director finally arrived, all became possible. The Director, Ahmid Mullah translated, wished to facilitate our progress, for we were guests of Afghanistan. Therefore, because of his great goodwill and generosity, he would provide us with enough coupons for the whole journey. We smiled, offered profuse thanks, made mental notes that where uniform administrative rules do not prevail or are only formal, the benefits of administration are not a matter of right, but a matter of the administrator's largesse.

After we had our coupons, Ahmid Mullah took us to the furrier. Our intention had been to pick up a spare fur cap or two for Sue's brothers, but when we arrived we found that such a cap is a very valuable item even here. Lloyd tried one — "I think my head is the size of Frank's" — and another and another. Our furrier's place was in the bazaar. (Bazaar means market, and usually consists of a street crowded with small stalls displaying their wares on sidewalk stands. The stores lock up late at night by folding up their stands and wares and closing up heavy wooden doors.) We pretty soon had a crowd of thirty or so silently watching as we bargained. Lloyd finally decided that a pale grey Karikul, prestige-wise certainly several notches above that of the Director of Rationing, would do for him! Sue mentally asked the brothers' pardon and we concentrated our bargaining on the chosen cap. "The color of the fur is poor!" "Who would possibly want such a cap?" "Look, the curl is imperfect in this place." We must not have been very convincing; we only got it down to 300 Afghanis ($9.00) from an original 350. Then we had no more Afghanis left, so the brothers got none. But the cold winter evenings in the US will be the better for it.

We left Herat around four in the afternoon, after paying Ahmid Mullah a commission for his services. We drove two hours, and finally made camp near a mountain stream below a splendid deserted fort. We had Wurst mit Selchbohnen and a splendid melon, then retired. We left two more melons, which had cost more than usual because of local crop failures, outside the car to cool. The night was uneventful, except for the comforting noises, heard around 2 a.m., of a sheep and goat herd grazing. A very quiet noise — one can hear them pulling up the grass.

August 16

We woke up at 5 a.m., to the extraordinary sight of five prostrate rears, some fifty yards from us in the direction of the creek. When we peeked through the curtains on the other three sides of the car, we discovered that another twenty to thirty turbaned men with long shirts were on their knees toward the rising sun. Further investigation through the curtains revealed a bus, i.e. a gaily painted, flower decorated truck which, like all the Afghan buses, carries people on its railed roof, where they seem to survive despite the blazing sun. The bus had stopped at the Fort, so that the passengers might wash in the creek, say their morning prayers, and visit the Fort. The latter must have provided facilities of more than historical interest. We lay low in our bed until the passengers reassembled. We didn't know if they'd appreciate our — especially Sue's — presence at their spiritual and other ablutions.

When they left, we climbed out, waited for the stream to clear itself, and did as they. We returned to the car in high spirits to enjoy our melons, unleavened bread and morning coffee. But, oh woe! The melons had disappeared. We have wondered ever since if the devout gentlemen or the goat herd stole them. But it was the only theft of the trip.

From Herat we went south to Farah — there is a northern and longer route, but it passes near the Russian border and the first consul in London specified in our passports that we go south. "We have a treaty . . . er . . . an agreement . . . er an understanding with the Russians that no Americans will go up that way." This is not strictly true, by the way. We know of several Americans who went the northern route about the time we were there, but the circumstances were exceptional. To go through Farah and Kandahar requires you to drive from the upper left hand corner of a quadrangle to the upper right via the lower left and right hand corners. There are lots of crows in Afghanistan, but no one flies as they do. The northern route, by the way, is just as far out of the way if not more.

We reached Farah around 1 p.m. The approach to it was rather magnificent: a huge old stone fort, with powerful round turrets stretching down in a way that suggests the fort once had a moat. The town itself consists of a main street and several desultory side-spurs. The hotel was another large, spacious building. The proprietor, who was sleeping on a rug on the floor in the front terrace, woke up because of the clamor the crowd gathering around us made. He chased away the importunate little boys, and led us down a long, shadowy hall to a room that was curtained off on the right.

We ordered omelet and melon and tea, and commiserated with one another concerning the steadily intensifying heat. At Farah it was hotter than at any time on our trip, and hotter than any day in Delhi subsequently, when we know the temperature passed 100. We estimate that Farah must have had 105—110 that day. Geographically this is easy to explain. The road which had come 200 kilometers or so south from Herat to Farah turns south-east here towards Kandahar. South of this road lies a desert which stretches flat and uninterrupted for many miles, and gives Farah the benefit of its dry heating capacity.

After lunch we tried to sleep, but the still, hot afternoon made the hours restless. At 4:30 we had another meal — a rice and meat pilaf — and at 5 p.m. we set off to tackle the desert road. We had been told that no one tackles it in the daytime, and we agree that no one should. Like all roads in Afghanistan, this one bounced us terribly. Shortly after we had negotiated a brief mountain pass which interrupted the otherwise straight and level road — and had almost impaled ourselves on the nose of an unlit truck parked well in the middle of the narrow mountain pass — Sue, who was driving, found that she couldn't control the steering wheel. Steering column broken! Disastrous damage to the alignment! Differential sick! Our first thoughts were all of major catastrophes, until Lloyd climbed out and announced a very flat tire.

It should be said that this was our first flat tire of the trip, caused in this case by a long horse-shoe nail. Nothing less could have gotten through our heavy-duty truck-style tires. The tire change took us almost an hour. The jack, which had been used only once before when Sue's uncle drove the car off that mountain side in Germany, was reluctant. We sweated over it, but couldn't get the darn thing to come down far enough to fit under the springs. We pulled out the "Proprietor's Manual" and the "Workshop Manual" of the Rover Company, peered at incomprehensible diagrams by the light of a tiny flashlight (the big one went on the blink just in time for this misadventure), sighed at the brilliant moon which lit the desert dramatically, encouraged ourselves with lukewarm tea made that morning, and fiddled with the jack. We were about to resign ourselves to wait-ing for the next truck — which might come in 5 minutes or 5 hours — when the jack suddenly decided to work. The rest was a cinch, and we continued.

This night's driving was a sheer endurance run. Fortunately no road between the Iranian and Pakistani border is comfortable enough to let one sleep, but on this pull we had trouble keeping our attention sharp. We looked for the bottle of Dexedrine that Ursula had given us for just this kind of emergency, but couldn't find it.

The road here was not just rough but downright treacherous — not as bad as it became after Kandahar, but bad enough. Afghanistan in the wet season has many freshets that rush down from the mountains into the level plains, and the flood bursts do not seem to be confined to streambeds. Everywhere we saw evidence that the waters wander reckless over the plains, eventually losing themselves in the desert. Many of the less temporary rivers of Afghanistan have no outlet to the sea. Even the Hari Rud, a mighty river in the wet season and a respectable one in the dry, loses itself in the sands of the southern desert. At their height, these rivers come tearing across the plain, and carry with them the stone bridges that cross the significant river beds. Once in Afghanistan we found three river beds in a row with their bridges intact, but this never happened again. The river beds vary in depth, and when a bridge is swept away the drop off may run to 10 or 20 feet. The drop offs are rarely marked — occasionally someone may have piled two stones on top of each other five yards from the critical point. Usually a track turns off some ten to thirty yards before the break, leads across the river bed and up on the other side. At night these places become a challenge: (a) to sight the drop in time; (b) to find the track; (c) to decide how deep the water is — when the river bed is wet; and (d) to find the track out on the other side.

Actually, we rarely had any trouble, and the challenge is more easily met than it sounds. But the possibilities for disaster are infinite. We would not have wanted to try these tracks with a car that had lower clearance than ours, or without four-wheel drive. On the other hand we saw or heard of Plymouths, Mercedes, Austins, Ford Populars and especially Volkswagens getting through — all with more trouble than we had. Broken springs were the most popular complaint, except on Volkswagens, plus tire blowouts and scraped and damaged bottoms.

The concept of a good road had become very relative for us. The Iranian roads were not good. They were dusty and often rough. But there was evidence of work on them. Every five miles or so, we would run across a father and son team, who often jumped up from where they slept by the side of the road when they sighted us in the distance, desultorily shoveling back into place the sand and gravel which the passage of cars had pushed to one side or another. They leveled the worst of the ruts and unevennesses, and marked all washouts with tidy little stonemen that provided quite adequate warning for alert drivers. Where the road was a washboard, and bounced us till our teeth rattled, we knew that if we could get over 25 mph the bump would even out. None of this was possible in Afghanistan. We will cheerfully endorse the estimate of those who told us that Afghanistan has the worst roads in the world! We haven't seen them all, of course.

We had two more adventures on this night journey. Lloyd had been following the road without difficulty out of a village and

down a short incline to a point where it began to parallel a river.
Suddenly and without warning — Lloyd had taken no bends or
turns — we were in sand half way up the wheels. While we were
prepared to expect the worst of the road, the dirt and gravel
had not before given way to sand. The car would move neither
forwards nor back. So we piled out, and in the pale moonlight
which was still with us began to investigate. We walked ahead to
where we hoped the sand would end, and the road begin again,
but found nothing but more sand. So we followed our track back
to where it disappeared on the hard rocks by the river side.
We made stale bad jokes which neither of us appreciated about
founding a new game called Find the Road. Eventually some
100 yards back we found the road, but it clearly led to the river
rocks which held no tracks. The question was, where did the road
continue? We flashed our tiny flashlight across the river to see
if this might be a ford, but could make out nothing since the river
was too wide. We then decided that we had better get the car out
first. The four-wheel drive, thank God, managed it after a few
false starts. When we turned the headlights toward the river, we
still could see no trace of road on the other side, and we could
not estimate the river's depth, but since we had exhausted the
alternatives, we decided to chance it. The car crossed alright, but
it took us another ten minutes before we found the road.

About 11 o'clock (it gets dark early in Afghanistan, at
about 6:30) we came to a village — i.e. a series of houses and
small shops along the road. The tea house looked inviting: two
winking lamps strung up above a huge copper samovar standing

in the open shop front, nearby a dark wooden rack with bright-colored teacups and teapots, some small Persian rugs on the floor near the samovar, and on one side five men in turbans sitting in a circle sipping tea. We parked and came over, requested chay. The proprietor, a young man, quickly brought the round pot (known as China in these parts, a splendid Persian word) and cups, a little bowl to put in tea leaves when you finished a cup, and a container of roughgrain sugar. The Afghans drink their tea by filling their cup half full of sugar, then pouring on tea from the little teapot, and drinking it without stirring. By the time the teapot is empty, the sugar is all gone too. While we drank — we found tea very invigorating when we were tired, day or night — we had a halting conversation with a bright eyed boy of perhaps ten whose name was Ali. We discussed distances to the next town, the names of various implements, and the weather. When we were ready to leave, Lloyd opened negotiations for payment, but one of the turbaned men rose and dismissed the possibility of payment. This would be a bakshish [tip] for us, he explained. We made grateful gestures and noises — one tries to use English even if one knows no one understands — and left.

At Girisk the road changed — suddenly at 4 a.m., when the darkness was lifting and we were tired to death of the driving, there appeared before us a well-graded, freshly graveled smooth road, with new bridges. This is the road that the Americans are said to have helped with, and we blessed American materialism with all our hearts as we sped along the next 60 miles to Kandahar at 50 mph.

We were in no condition to appreciate Kandahar when we arrived, though it is certainly a charming city — with big, low yellow stucco buildings set in gardens that struggle to survive the heat.

We found the Kandahar hotel, another gaily painted stucco structure, and were received by a rather inept manager in western bush-shirt and trousers, with western pretensions but no real feeling for hospitality. Our ruder hosts at Farah and Herat were much nicer. He couldn't make up his mind for a while whether he could really serve us lunch already at 11 o'clock. (We had had no full meal since the previous afternoon.) Once he made up his mind to do so, the food was unattractively served — even by our now modest standards. We slept until about 4 p.m., and then Lloyd went out with one of the hotel employees to get the tire fixed. Meanwhile, Sue met three people in the lobby, all of whom spoke German. They asked if Lloyd and I would take one of them, a tall Austrian young man with a fish-belly colored, unappealing appearance to Kabul. He was a professional world traveler, on the road one year already and financing himself with the proceeds of lectures and slide showings. Subsequently he brought out a large scrapbook in which were displayed pictures of himself with "significant" personalities around the world. "Here I am with the Chief Police Inspector of Baghdad." "Here I am with Ibn Saud's son." "Here I am on Radio Cairo."

We had discovered, by the way, that there are numerous types of world travelers. But there seems to be one kind that

90

makes all embassies from Yugoslavia to Kabul flinch. He is the fellow on his way around the world on $15.00, and here he is in Meshed, half way round, and he still has $13.00. There are surely some fine men among these, but the typical example seems to feel that because he has been brave or harebrained enough to attempt this extraordinary adventure, he can expect all Europeans along the way to meet all his demands, outrageous and otherwise. The embassies further east, where the going is tough, seem to have had their fill of such types. We found some consular and embassy officials very wary when we first met them to ask for local advice. They all relaxed and turned out to be warm and helpful eventually, but only after they found we were not expecting them to supply food, lodging, gas and guide service free of charge. The Yale group which came through last summer, though they were probably not of the $15.00 variety, made a poor impression by being rude about insisting on gas at the Kabul Embassy as a matter of right, and not paying for it (or not paying adequately, we are not sure which).

In any case, Sue put off the world traveler, hoping for Lloyd's return and a bolder refusal. We picked up riders several times on our trip, but except for the Turk who went with us to Trabzon, we never took any one for long distances. It would be a good man whom one could like after a day of heat on those terrible roads. The ride to Kabul was overnight besides, and we didn't relish the prospect of having to search for accommodations for a third person, when we could simply stop anywhere. Meanwhile the Austrian further endeared himself to Sue by some authoritative

lecturing on the atrocities which the Americans had committed
against the Germans during the Second World War.

Another man in the lobby turned out to be the director of
a documentary the Russians were making on Afghanistan.
Lourou had won the Stalin Prize for camera work, and was
reconnoitering for the film. His companion was an Afghan
named Nasseri, a tall, mustachioed, handsome man who was
assistant to the editor of the leading Kabul newspaper. He was
guiding Lourou on behalf of the government as far as we could
make out. He lectured Sue warmly on the Pashtoonistan issue,
and explained that the floods which had ravaged Afghanistan
earlier in the year were only to be expected in view of US and
Russian atomic experiments. Kasseri had taken a PhD in
journalism from Munich, was a charming, emotional, intelligent
and slightly superstitious man.

While she waited, Sue began to discuss the route from
Kandahar to Kabul with Lourou. It turned out that he and
Nasseri were traveling the same way as we, and also leaving
in an hour. Apparently the Austrian had tried to get a ride
with them, and they were wishing him on to us. Lourou was
helpful about the road, and went off to fetch a Russian map
of Afghanistan, which he apparently considered more helpful
than the local product. He invited Sue to a couch across the
room to inspect the map, and in the course of the next half hour
revealed himself as a rather gentle, pleasant bourgeois, who was
delighted to find someone who would commiserate with him on
Afghanistan's inconveniences. "I left for this trip on my twenty-

fifth anniversary and I thought I might have my wife follow me. I thought Kabul would be a modern city, but one cannot even get a safe glass of water." He and Sue compared Karakul prices, because he wanted to buy a coat for his daughter who is studying medicine. Sue asked him about the occasions he was photographing, and he implied that there wasn't really enough to fill an hour and a half documentary. He added in an aside that one couldn't, after all, simply take pictures of monuments — apparently that is what the Afghans would have preferred.

Lloyd returned finally with a young German in tow who was going around the world the other way and who was obviously not relaxing and enjoying it. On the bus from Pakistan into Afghanistan he had heard that a German doctor had recently been stabbed on the streets of Herat, that a Russian who nudged a pedestrian with his bicycle in Kabul was slain by the victim, and that Afghanistan was, all in all, not a safe place. He had been robbed of a suitcase in Calcutta (he gave one of two suitcases to each of two men, and when both ran away he could only chase one), robbed by porters from Patna to Peshawar, and was finding the East a terrible trial. One has the feeling that some of the professional world travelers are types who have never been able to control their universe anywhere, and then are surprised that they can't manipulate the new environment they have sought as an escape from the old. (Department of glittering generalization.) We felt immensely superior.

At five we left for Kabul, ahead of the film car which had finally agreed to take the Austrian. The road from Kandahar to

Ghazni was almost the worst we encountered — more dangerous
because of deep and frequent bridge washouts. We drove until
twelve, when we were exhausted, and bedded down on the seats
without even making up the bed in the back. Around two we
heard the film car go by.

August 18

After a melon breakfast, we started on the last lap of the journey at five in the morning. After only an hour's drive, we were
flagged down by the Austrian, who was looking even paler than
usual. For a moment we entertained the thought that he had
been left behind by Louvou and Kasseri, but we soon discovered
that instead the whole party had suffered a small disaster.
The Afghan driver had been tired, and around 2:30 a.m., he
had almost failed to see a deep drop off in the road. He had
stopped only three feet short of the plunge — we could see the
tire marks. He had then looked for the by-pass and mistaken a
nearby sandy descent for the makeshift road. Result: the car, a
1947 Plymouth stationwagon, ground into the sand and could
go neither forward nor back. They had tried for two hours to
push it out, and then slept fitfully on the ground around it for
another hour. About the time of our own arrival, two nomads
arrived on the scene, and with the additional manpower the car
came out.

We let them go ahead, which was well enough since they soon
ran aground again. At 7 a.m., we found them in a dry river bed,

trying hopelessly to start the car with the hand starter. They explained that the motor had conked out when they came down the incline into the river bed, just after they hit an obstruction. Lloyd inquired if they had inspected the underside of the vehicle. No, they hadn't thought of that. Good idea. It turned out that the gear-box had been damaged and the gears locked. Lovrov, pale from the night's exertion, glanced nervously from time to time at a sad sight nearby: a large truck, with its motor completely removed, sat on the hill overlooking the sick Plymouth. Its cargo was guarded by two desolate Afghans, who had been waiting for two weeks for the return of the motor, which had gone to Kabul for repairs.

We waited around for an hour, until it became plain that the Plymouth would recover, and then we went ahead.

We met the film party again in a town some two hours further on. It caught up with us as we were replenishing our gas supply, and Nasseri invited us for breakfast. The town's only "Hotel" had a large room, empty of furniture except for a large rug. We sat on the floor and were served an inexhaustible supply of boiled eggs and tea, and recuperated.

At noon, we met again for the last time at Ghazni, the home of Mahmoud, the great invader of India. The film expedition was going to stop there and sleep for the afternoon, but we pushed on to Kabul, which we reached after dark. A soldier whom we asked the way to the American Embassy — we already knew that the Kabul Hotel was full, occupied by the Russian soccer team — promptly jumped in the car and personally guided us the four or five miles. He refused to take any money.

The marine guard at the Embassy told us that possibly the ICA staff house might have some room, but he couldn't raise them by phone. He then directed us to the house of Hugh Pettys, who worked on Communications for the Embassy (we never were able to find out the significance of Communications) and to whom we had an introduction from the Cochranes at the Meshed Mission. The Pettys were out. We were already getting ready to pull the curtains and sleep in the streets of Kabul, when it occurred to us to ask the Pettys servant for directions to the ICA staff house. He gave some rather general ones, and we started prowling up and down alleys looking for it. Just as we were about to give up in a new burst of desperation, we heard laughing and English voices down the street — a somewhat entwined western couple, who turned out to be young UNESCO personnel. They knew where the staff house was and took us there. It lay behind a high wall, the door of which was opened by an uncommunicative Afghan. The UNESCO girl, who turned out to be endowed with limitless brass, commanded him to admit us all, and strode into the attractive building with all the confidence of an owner. "Where was the manager?" she inquired. "Miss Poindexter is asleep." (It was then 8:30.) "Wake her up!" "Oh no madame. Miss Poindexter would kill me." "Well then, which of your rooms is empty? Where can these people sleep?"

The servant reluctantly allowed that one room was empty. Our intrepid friend inspected it critically, and conceded that it might be alright for us. (Best place we'd seen since Teheran.) She then ordered the servant into the kitchen to prepare tea sandwiches, and after having quieted our misgivings about crashing the house this way, swept off gaily with her more diffident young man.

August 19

Our stay at the "plantation" was very pleasant, although we never did quite know what our status there was until the very end, when we were charged $16.00 for the two days. Miss Poindexter, a well-dressed southern spinster of around 40 who had been meant for something better than the secretarial position she held at the Embassy, was the reason for the nickname of the staff house. She referred to it as "my home" sufficiently frequently that we were even more doubtful about our status there than when we arrived. The charge that we finally paid included meals, but except for the first morning breakfast our meal status was also never clear. We had the impression that Miss Poindexter had never come to terms with the fact that she managed something other than her own house.

We mailed out some postcards, changed more money, and had lunch with the Hugh Pettyses, who were very nice to us. In addition, we took the Land-Rover over to a TCM man who was teaching in an American financed technical school. Poor Rover! After all his faithful service, an extra high road obstruction the night before had knocked something loose below and he was losing oil while Lloyd drove. Sue had spent some hours with the shop manual looking at pictures ("Drive shaft screw B may be lubricated by dismantling Fitting C and opening Slot X") and had concluded that the damaged part was the plate on the emergency brake cylinder, which resides next to the gearbox. Her analysis was correct, but we had also lost the seal on the gearbox. The TCM man said we would have no trouble getting to the Land-Rover dealer in Lahore — fortunate, because major and even minor repairs in Kabul take weeks and may not be adequate.

While passing through the Embassy that afternoon, we picked up their daily newssheet, and discovered that Emily Kruger, old friend of the Hoebers, former boss to Sue during a college summer job, and opinion pollster extraordinary for the State Department, was up in Kabul feeling out Afghan opinion of the American exhibit at the big industries fair. We had a joyful reunion and made a date to see the American exhibit that night.

Meanwhile we had cocktails at his beautiful house with Steve Baldanza, the bouncy and witty Embassy Public Affairs Officer who was interested in our trip. Baldanza has been married for 13 years, and has just sent his wife, pregnant for the first time, to Europe to have her baby. He credits the mountain air with the event. He also explained that he decided to send his wife away after a TCM official two weeks earlier had had to deliver his own child with his right hand while turning over the pages of a "Do It Yourself" pamphlet with the left. The two or so doctors in town had been busy at the crucial hour. The medical facilities are still fairly primitive, and emergencies must still be flown out on navy planes at staggering costs to the ill man.

In Kabul, we pieced together most of the story of the tragic Winant case, which had haunted us from Salzburg. We picked up the rest of the tale at the Pakistan border, in Delhi, and even in Jaipur.

Photo of our Land Rover at Jai Mahal Palace Hotel, Jaipur 1956.

In Salzburg we heard that Peter Winant, nephew of the late US Ambassador to Great Britain who committed suicide, and a Swedish girl traveling with him, had disappeared without a trace on the Northern route through Afghanistan. In Meshed, the vice-consul had just returned from an unsuccessful trip into northern Afghanistan to trace the couple. And in Kabul, Steve Baldanza had just received proofs of a reward poster with pictures of the couple which would be distributed throughout the north.

We don't know quite how reliable all our material is, but this is what we pieced together. Winant was said to have cut himself loose from his rather wealthy parents at the age of eighteen, refusing thereafter to receive money from them, and seeking to build a rather different life for himself. He was apparently brilliant — "He taught himself Persian while crossing Afghanistan before" — and introverted. He cycled alone across Afghanistan on his way to India. One of the Kabul Embassy people, driving from Kandahar to Kabul, overtook him along the way, and amazed and surprised at the sight of a lonely westerner, shouted an enthusiastic greeting. "Hi," said Winant, and cycled on. When some ten days later, the official returned to Kandahar on the same route, he again met the lone cyclist, and greeted him with enthusiasm. "Hi," responded Winant, and continued, unperturbed.

In India, Winant worked with Vinobha Bhave, the Gandhian disciple who initiated the great Land-gift Movement. The Pakistan border officials, who remembered him, said his passport described him as a missionary.

His companion, the Swedish girl [later identified as Gunna Gumeson], was apparently in her middle twenties, attractive, blonde and blue-eyed. The Jesuit Fathers at Jaipur remembered her. She had worked in the villages on a kind of private mission work. Like Winant, she apparently had no affiliation with an organized religious group. She would go out to the villages with a bearer and some Indian women, and work at educating the village women on hygiene and health. She also seems to have worked with Bhave — possibly that is where they met.

They must have decided to return to Europe together, via the Northern route in Afghanistan. The fact that they were plainly unmarried caused some gossip among those who had not met them, but those that had generally agreed that the relationship must have been Platonic. The Pakistan border officials described him as shoeless, wearing a long Indian shirt and trousers. She also wore some simple white garment. The officials offered them some roasted chicken, but they declined. Winant said that the bread and water diet was better for them on the road. They walked into Afghanistan, hitching rides along the way. In Kabul, the Embassy tried to dissuade them from taking the Northern route in their unprotected, vehicle-less condition, and to persuade Winant to put on shoes. Neither argument was successful. The last westerners to see them, an Austrian family up north with a firm that is constructing a factory, said Winant's feet were bloody when they arrived there.

They left Kabul in May, with very little money and a determination to ask for food and shelter from people along the way, rather like wandering monks. Winant's parents knew of their departure because they, it is said, arranged to get reports on his whereabouts from the various embassies, a task that was presumably eased by the family's foreign service connections. The Winants, having heard nothing more, eventually wrote the Meshed consulate asking if their son had been through there. The consulate replied that they'd seen nothing of him, and began to investigate. This was early in July, and the trail must have been very cold already. Nevertheless, the Embassy apparatus on the one hand and the Afghan official agencies on the other immediately went into high gear. The Kabul Chief of Police personally conducted the investigation in the north, and when we were in Kabul, two hundred people were said to be in prison on suspicion.

Meanwhile the Winants arrived in Kabul, and Winant senior set out with Christie Wilson, chaplain to the western protestant community in Kabul, to follow the trail. The most recent piece of information available was that they had been last picked up by a truck driver, and not seen thereafter. When we reached Delhi we heard that the truck driver had been found and told of leaving them at a crossroads of which one road led north into Russia and the other west to Persia.

Two theories were held at Kabul: one, that he had been slain for her and she carried off to the brown tents in which the nomads live. We saw the nomad colonies on the move, with an elder leading out front, the heavily laden camels lumbering in line with poultry perched on top, and the women in their brilliant clothes and bangles bringing up the rear. A blonde woman would be much prized there, and among the ever moving tribes she would be hard to find. The other theory was that they had both gone north, to see Russia. We never heard the end of the story.

While this tale was no comfort to us on our travels, we never ran the risks they did. Travelers on foot who beg their way and give the impression of poverty and helplessness are a more vulnerable target, according to Kabulians, than travelers in a well-equipped vehicle who look as though they have recently been seen by civilization and obviously are prosperous enough that the forces of law and order would take an interest in them. The Afghans have made the Winant case their special concern because the disappearance makes their land seem wild and uncivilized. They are striving hard to extend law and order, and this case has been a blow to their prestige.

Our last evening at Kabul was spent with Emily Kruger at the Industries Fair. We saw the US shell, an aluminum and plastic bubble that had been flown in and put up in a day, to the amazement of the other, mostly satellite and Russian exhibitors. The Fair was not yet open, and the occasion of our visit was a preview for the Afghan Communications Minister (and censor) of a US documentary on Afghanistan. To the profound embarrassment of Steve Baldanza, who was shepherding the minister, the American generator broke down. Doubly embarrassing was the fact that it had been brought in partially to ensure that a failure of Kabul's electricity would not throw the US exhibit into darkness.

Steve, after running out of conversation of his own, brought the minister over to us, and we occupied him with questions on

Afghan history, while people rushed to and fro procuring "lots of kilowatts." The generator flatly refused to come back to life, the minister went home, and we all went to Steve's where we consumed more good liquor.

August 20

We had promised ourselves that the arrival in Peshawar would be considered the official end of our journey. The last lap was easy. The road from Kabul to Peshawar is much better than roads anywhere else in the country. This was just as well, because we wasted half a day getting gas for the remaining 250 or so miles. The Herat coupons were not acceptable to Kabulians. The last stretch is very attractive — instead of the flat, high plateau we finally found mountains. We followed the roaring Kabul river, a joy to our eyes after the dry 2000 miles before.

We reached the Pakistan border at seven, when it legally closes, but border officials gave us sweet green tea and let us go on, along the marvelous black top road which starts immediately on the other side of the Afghan border. They provided us with a guard from the border constabulary, a tough looking Pathan in khaki shorts and shirt, a decorated turban, bearing a rifle with fixed bayonet. Since the car was full, he had to climb in next to Sue, which he accomplished after a first attempt to climb with his heavy boots on the seat and into the back. Through the Khyber, which takes a half an hour to cross, and into Peshawar, he kept his heavy foot resolutely on Sue's sandaled foot oblivious of her kicks at his ankle.

The Khyber is still not entirely safe, and frequently constabulary check points have been erected to assure that no traveler is picked off by a roaring frontier tribe.

Out of the pass we emerged into the flatlands below, which looked more rich and fruitful in the dark than anything we had known since the Black Sea. Here and there, we saw signs of a highly organized society, compared to those we had left: the cantonment signs, the Civil Lines, the sign "Government High School," the blacktop roads, the sign to the railway retiring room, the little officialisms in language that showed the English stamp. We almost had tears in our eyes, and did not condemn completely the colonialism which had left such comforting signs.

We drove straight to Dean's Hotel, a hotel in the British-Indian tradition, with fans, and dressing rooms, and flush toilets that worked, and a six course menu. We were received into the gentle arms of a colonial-influenced civilization by 5 white-turbaned hotel servants. When the dessert, an English sweet, was brought on, and the tea was served with a pitcher of hot milk, we drank to England and to Pakistan and celebrated our emergence from the underdeveloped areas into the developed Indian sub-continent.

Appendix I
Shopping List for Permanent Provisions

two plastic plate and
cup sets

three assorted carving knives

one cork screw

one can opener

two knives, fork and spoon
sets

three plastic screw-top
containers

one plastic egg carrier

one large and two small
plastic storage jars

plastic salt and pepper
shakers

one large pot

set of three cooking pots,
frying-pan and teapot

one folding table

two folding chairs

one rubber basin

one nylon clothesline

thirty plastic clothespins

two scrub pads

two heavy quality, large
plastic bags (for laundry,
other uses)

one large and one small
flashlight, with batteries and
extra bulbs

one plastic table cloth

two dozen assorted sized
plastic bags
one ashtray
one shaving mirror
one plastic toothbrush glass
one hand broom
two egg cups
one cutting board
two pot holders
one can of Flit
package of rubber bands
two warm woolen blankets
two lightweight cotton
blankets
one canvas bag to hold the
blankets

four Turkish towels
four wash rags (type that fit
over the hand, more convenient
for bathtubless washing)
muslin curtains for the car
two small pillows
two muslin sheets
four pillows cases
two dish rags
three dish towels
one cotton apron
two rolls of paper towels, four
rolls toilet paper
two boxes paper napkins
four light but absorbing
novels*

*Saraband For Dead Lover, by Helen Simpson; The Nightcomers, by Eric Ambler; Nightrunners of Bengal, by John Masters; The Judas Window, by Carter Dickson. The Masters and the Ambler were poor choices, since they dealt with danger in foreign lands, splendid by the cozy fireplace, but hair-raising when you are parked below a barren hill in Afghanistan, and the noises of the night are all around.

All this equipment should be much more securely fastened in the car than we managed to fasten it. Ropes and storage boxes into which the equipment can be tightly packed should be added to the list.

Appendix II
Pre-Trip Expenses for Travelers to India

1) Pre-trip expenses that might be incurred, by travelers to India regardless of means of transportation (for two people)

Two passports	$20.00
Visa and Passport pictures	$22.00
Inoculations	$16.75
Visas for two for India	$ 5.00
Cable to get India visa for one year in a hurry (unsuccessful)	$20.00
Insurance	
Health Insurance, for one year, for two	$158.00
Theft Insurance	$35.00
Drugs	$25.00
	$301.75

2) Special pre-trip expenses Incurred because of motor trip

Triptique	$50.00
Insurance for car[*]	$252.00
British Licenses[**]	$1.50
British War Office Maps	$15.00
Equipment for trip[***]	$60.00
Visas for two[****]	
Afghanistan	$3.50
Yugoslavia	$ 2.00
	$384.00

[*] For one year (would have been incurred whether we drove or not if we used a car in India)

[**] International license may be procured at no extra cost with Triptique and Insurance

[***] See Appendix I

[****] No charge for European countries, Greece, Turkey, Iran, and Pakistan

Appendix III

Expenditures by Country and Expenditure by Topic

(in dollars)

	Austria	Yugos-lavia	Greece	Turkey	Iran	Afghan-istan	Total
Food and supplies for trip	7.15	3.76	.87	8.20	15.62	1.96	37.56
Food eaten out	3.00	3.90	4.35	5.50	5.05	—	21.80
Gas	10.12	25.25	14.65	22.95	22.90	16.86	112.73
Hotels	—	2.00	—	13.00	27.00	22.25	64.25
Car service & repairs	8.00	5.00	—	8.00	9.10	—	30.10
Mail	.21	.75	—	.90	1.00	2.00	4.89
Other	1.80	—	1.40	.10	11.85	10.75	25.90
Total	30.31	40.66	21.27	58.65	92.52	53.82	297.23

Writing India[1]
A Career Overview

Previously published in *India Review*, vol. 7, no. 4
(October–December 2008), pp. 266–94.

Our academic careers began roughly 50 years ago when we arrived in India in 1956 with two Ford Foundation Foreign Area Training Fellowships to study politics in Rajasthan and Tamil Nadu. Our teaching careers came to a close at the University of Chicago on April 2003 with a Festschrift conference on "Area Studies Redux: Situating Knowledge in a Globalizing World." These two singular moments in our academic lives emphasize that "area studies" were central to our inquiries about India and the discipline of Political Science. "Area" as a geographic and cultural concept encompassed several levels of inquiry: on the one hand "India," with its immense diversity, on the other a region such as "Rajasthan," or "Madras," with their more particular cultural scene.

114   Area studies captures a central tendency of the method and substance of our work on Indian politics. Our early take on area studies is indicated by the title of the book we wrote on the basis of the research we conducted in 1956 and 1957, *The Modernity of Tradition*.[2] Unlike the view of the then-regnant modernization theory—that tradition would be swept into the dustbin of history and that "they" were destined to become like "us"—we found that tradition was often adaptive, change dialectical, not dichotomous, and that "we" could learn from "them."

In the *Modernity of Tradition*'s introduction we warned readers about "the imperialism of categories and historical possibilities." Was a prosperous middle class, as Seymour Martin Lipset held, a "requisite of democracy" in India?[3] Could social change in India be explained by the dichotomous "pattern variables" posited by Edward Shils and Talcott Parsons[4] or captured by structural-functional variables posited by Gabriel Almond?[5] We took an alternative view in *The Modernity of Tradition*. Change in India, we found, could be best understood as adaptations of a complex and variegated traditional society and culture.

Almost 50 years later, at the "Area Studies Redux" conference held at the University of Chicago in April 2003, we revisited area studies[6] by confronting issues raised by global processes and formal modes of inquiry. September 11, 2001 had challenged America's parochialism by reminding it that the country lived in a diverse and complex world but lacked adequate means to grasp its meanings. The events of 9/11 brought to the fore the realization that knowledge of the other's languages, ways of life and world views mattered for America's security and prosperity. Instead of asking "Why can't they be more like us," Americans should be asking, "What can we learn about them and how can we live with difference?"

Long before 9/11 challenged American parochialism, some social scientists had begun to bypass area studies in favor of using data sets to test formal models statistically and run "large-n" country studies. As Princeton History Professor Stephen Kotkin put it in a *New York Times* article of September 7, 2002, if you tried to find

> a full-time political scientist who specializes in the Middle East or South Asia at the nation's universities, you'd almost be out of luck. The absence of regional experts in political science departments of many elite universities goes back to long-running, rancorous debate over the best method for understanding the way the world works: is it using statistics and econometrics to identify universal patterns that underlie all economic and political systems, or zeroing in on a particular area and mastering its languages, cultures and institutions?

By 2003 we had come to understand area studies knowledge as situated knowledge,[7] knowledge that is located and marked by time and place and circumstance.

116 It is unlike the objective knowledge on offer by those who adhere to a universal social science epistemology, an epistemology based on the obsolete methods of Newtonian science that purports to be true everywhere and always. Unlike such theory-driven, universal social science knowledge, area studies knowledge tends to be problem-driven and more prone to inductive generalization than to deductive reasoning.

In 1956 we had recently finished our degrees at Harvard. We were among the first generation of American scholars to do research in post-colonial India. We purchased a Land Rover for delivery in London and set off in mid-July on an overland journey across Europe to Turkey, Iran and Afghanistan, crossing into the Indian sub-continent over the Khyber Pass to Peshawar, traveling through the Punjab to Lahore and Amritsar, and then on to New Delhi and Jaipur, the capital city of Rajasthan in India's northwest.

During six months of research in Jaipur we lived with the multi-generational, joint family of a large Rajput landlord. He hosted assemblies of Rajput nobility and princes as they decided on their response to the disempowering of the princely order and land reform. We imagined we were witness to the abolition of the old order. We struck roots and made friends.[8] In February we traveled overland by Land Rover to Madras in southeast India. We were committed to learning about India's South as well as its North, and British as well as princely India.

1956/57 was the first and 1999/2000 the last of
11 years spent in India doing academic research. Starting
in 1962/63 with the first of our three children, we took
them along. They attended Jaipur schools—Maharani
Gayatri Devi Girls Public School ("MGD") (the girls),
and St. Xaviers (the boy). They went on to duplicate a Raj/
English colonial experience, attending Woodstock School,
a missionary-founded boarding school in the lower
Himalayas, where they made friends, competed in sports
and learned Hindi.

Our writing about India wandered beyond the boundaries of our "native place," political science. It is another
virtue of the emphasis on area studies that it invites a
multi-disciplinary approach; we took full advantage of
this feature. From time to time we have drawn on history, sociology, anthropology and literary criticism to
explore problems that interest us. Our writing about
India has addressed the following topics which we discuss
below: modes of inquiry; theorizing politics and society;
Occidentalism and Orientalism; processes of state formation; processes of institutional change; identity politics;
making US foreign policy; writing as public intellectuals.

Modes of Inquiry

Our methodological evolution began with a 1958
article in *Public Opinion Quarterly*. The article analyzed

the results of one of the first random sample surveys done in India. Carried out in the state of Madras, it examined the relationship between media exposure and political attitudes. Our field experience led us to raise questions about the methodological individualist assumptions of opinion and electoral research. Among our last published articles on modes of inquiry are essays in a volume edited by Kristen Monroe[9] on the pluralist challenge by the Perestroika movement to efforts within the American Political Science Association to establish the hegemony of formal modeling, rational choice and large-n studies.

Many of our essays reflect the changing landscape of our relationship to modes of inquiry. All reflect our concern to give priority to questions over methods, a concern which privileges induction over deduction and pluralism over monopoly.

The two oldest essays, "Surveys in India" (1958)[10] and "Determinants and Varieties of Agrarian Mobilization" (1984),[11] were written under the influence of a behavioral social science that attempts to use independent variables to explain dependent variables. "Surveys" was a response to India's second general election under universal suffrage in 1957. In the absence of survey research, little was known about voters' political knowledge, attitudes and preferences. We designed and tested a survey and recruited, trained and supervised the team of ten interviewers that carried it out among a 600-person random sample of voters in Madras state.[12] In the context of low literacy, our study related demographic variables and levels and types of media exposure to political attitudes and party preferences.

We discovered that the assumption, embedded in American survey research methods, that the individual was the basic unit of opinion was invalid in the Indian context. Many respondents did not know what their opinion was until they had discussed the question in a family or village context. The group was the basic unit.

"Determinants" tries inter alia to unravel the conundrum of structure versus agency by asking how objective determinants or "causes" and subjective determinants or "reasons" relate to collective action. The literature on agrarian radicalism suggested that desperate objective conditions did not readily translate into action because the meaning and consequences of adverse objective conditions were neither self-evident to actors nor self-executing. Whether objective conditions matter for collective action depends, we argued, on how well leaders are able to translate causes into reasons.

Our more recent articles, "Engaging Subjective Knowledge" (2003), "The Imperialism of Categories" (2005), "Perestroika and Its Other" (2005) and "Let a Hundred Flowers Bloom" (2005), are concerned with epistemology and heuristics.[13] They were written in part in the context of the Perestroika movement's efforts to counter the claims of those advocating a singular "scientific method" for political science.

The millennium witnessed the onset of a *Methoden Streit* in the American Political Science Association. An anonymous voice calling him/her/themselves "Perestroika" challenged the hegemonic pretensions of rational choice, formal modeling and large-n studies in the name of methodological pluralism. The contestation took place on a list-serve which, at its height, approximated 800 voices. We were actively engaged in the movement.

"Engaging Subjective Knowledge" questions the claim that the objective, universal knowledge produced by an obsolete version of Newtonian science, knowledge that is said to be true everywhere and always, is the only form of valid knowledge. We make the case for the validity of the subjective, partial and contingent knowledge found in Amar Singh's first-person diary narrative. Amar Singh tells "what he knows" rather than the truth, the whole truth and nothing but the truth.

In "The Imperialism of Categories," Susanne Rudolph addressed the politics of concept formation and use. Categories of the rich and powerful West were thought to have global reach and relevance. The imperial center instructed the colonial periphery about what questions to ask and how to answer them. Modernization theory taught that there were stages of development that would enable them to become like us.

For some political scientists "theorizing politics and society" is an oxymoron. Victoria Hattam, writing as President of Politics and History, an Organized Section of the American Political Science Association, deplored the "deep and enduring" split between theory and empirical research in political science. Behavioral political scientists, she said, had no use for theorists and theorists no use for the scientific pretensions of behaviorists. She argues that a tacit compromise was forged in the 1960s that exempted theorists from the strictures of behavioralist methodological critiques and left empirical political science supposedly devoid of larger theoretical ambition ... The discipline's flagship journal, the *American Political Science Review*, reflected the compromise when issue after issue contained a slate of behavioral articles accompanied by a single theory essay.[14]

Perhaps because she was writing from the enclave of Americanist studies, Hattam found that the split leaves "no space for the kind of work I aspire to." We experienced the split Hattam recently deplored but not the disempowerment she experienced. Our teachers and, subsequently, colleagues at Harvard, Carl Friedrich, Samuel Beer and Louis Hartz, used theory to frame and analyze historical and empirical questions. We learned too from David Riesman and Eric Erikson that theory, social and psychological as well as political, helped to identify and answer questions. By 1964, when we left Harvard for the University of Chicago, we often found that Max Weber's ideal typical mode of theorizing was a good starting point for research and analysis. At the University of Chicago theory mattered in the intense discussions of the Committee on the Comparative Study of New Nations. Like M. Jourdain in Moliere's *Bourgeois Gentilhomme* who was surprised to learn that he was speaking prose, we were surprised to find that we were speaking theory.

Between 1961 and 2001 we wrote eight articles that theorized institutional change. They deal with the construction and meaning of political culture and the interpretation and explanation of social change and social structure. The first article, Susanne Rudolph's 1961 "Consensus and Conflict in Indian Politics,"[15] along with work by W. H. Morris-Jones and Myron Weiner[16] began the analysis of how political culture in India could be derived and how it could shape and constrain Indian political institutions and behavior.

Two articles, our introduction to *The Modernity of Tradition* and our revisionist interpretation of Weber on bureaucracy, deal with social change and social structures. In the introduction to *The Modernity of Tradition*[17] we argue that social change in India was characterized more by adaptation of tradition than its eradication. In so far as we have made an impression on the social sciences, this introduction was probably the most influential. It was published at a moment when modernization theory was hegemonic, and challenges to it seemed imprudent. In the event, the book achieved some traction; forty years after it was first published, it is still in print. In our 1979 critique of Weber's construction of bureaucratic rationality and efficiency we argued that he failed to take account of the existence and effects of power inside and outside bureaucratic organizations that vitiate the operation of a purely rationalist bureaucratic ethos.[18] And we called attention to the persistence of patrimonial features, such as loyalty and affect, that, we argue, promote rather than block organizational effectiveness.

In the 1990s political scientists were rediscovering and resuscitating civil society as an antidote to state-centric political science and touting it as a necessary condition for the success of democracy and market economies in developing societies. Susanne Rudolph's article "Civil Society and the Realm of Freedom"[19] challenged such broad claims. Differentiating civil society's meanings and contexts, she argued that non-state actors can be un-civil as well as civil. Indian colleagues were, at the same time, producing studies of Indian rural communities that showed dysfunctional aspects of civil society.[20] Civil society formations included not only voluntary associations and NGOs that produce social capital and trust but also criminal and violent drug mafias, terrorist organizations and youth

124   gangs. And associational life can produce self-seeking and debilitating conflict as well as deliberation and the public good.

Lloyd Rudolph's 1992 article "The Media and Cultural Politics"[21] was written after the end of Congress party dominance and at the beginning of a multi-party system, coalition governments, and the deregulation of television broadcasting. It was a time of marked expansion in the number of television viewers. Political communication was shifting from local speech and print media to electronic media, particularly television.

The article explores the rise, meaning and early consequences of media-driven cultural politics in India. The move from print to television in a country still two-thirds illiterate, particularly the debut of television mega-series starting with the *Ramayana*, riveted the nation, shifting public attention to culturally iconic high culture and away from village-level versions of folk culture. The early TV mega-series willy-nilly helped to standardize the meaning of Hinduism as a public culture and opened the way to the formation of a Hindu national identity.

Occidentalism and Orientalism

Two articles, "Occidentalism and Orientalism"[22] and "Living with Difference,"[23] arose out of a request in 1995 by the then editor of *Comparative Studies in Society and*

History (*CSSH*) Raymond Grew, and by Sally Humphrey, editor of a volume commissioned by *CSSH*, reflexively to examine our 1965 *CSSH* article "Barristers and Brahmins: Legal Cultures and Social Change." Thirty years on, how would we revise the article in the light of changes in the "culture of scholarship," i.e. the paradigms and research methodologies in which the subject was embedded in 1965?

"Occidentalism and Orientalism" and "Living with Difference" were responses to the question posed by Grew and Humphrey. Perhaps the most important change in the culture of scholarship between 1965 and 1995 was the rise of an "Orientalist" epistemology. The articles gave us an opportunity to intervene in the debate that was roiling the academy: whether, as Edward Said argued in *Orientalism* (1978),[24] knowledge of the Oriental other produced by Western scholars was to be discounted because those who produced it were motivated by the power requirements of colonial rule.

Said's *Orientalism* seemed to establish a watershed for how to read Western, particularly British, scholarship about India. Said's epistemological claims led us to reconsider inter alia the motives and scholarship of the first generation of East India Company scholars who brought knowledge of India's civilizational texts to the attention of European and American intellectuals. In characterizing those East India Company scholars, had not Saidians themselves engaged in a reverse Orientalism, an occidentalism[25] that de-historicized, stereotyped and essentialized the knowledge they produced?

We argued that an effect of "Orientalist" scholarship was to break through the European belief that Greco-Roman civilization was singular by recognizing that there were other great civilizations. We sought to illustrate the deficiency of a Saidian construction of the early "Orientalists" by re-examining the career and scholarship of Sir William Jones, a high court judge in the Bengal presidency of the East India Company when Warren Hastings was Governor General. He records in his diary his recognition of and appreciation for the accomplishments and virtues of three great civilizations other than his own Greco-Roman one, the Arabic, the Persian and the Indian. They are: "the scene of glorious actions, fertile in the productions of human genius, abounding in natural wonders, infinitely diversified in the form of religion and government, in the laws, manners, customs and languages, as well as in the feature and complections [sic] of men."[26]

Soon after his arrival in Calcutta, Jones established a learned society, the Asiatic Society of Bengal.[27] He and his Asiatic Society colleagues, Henry T. Colebroke, James Prinsep, Charles Wilkins, and Nathaniel Halhed, learned the languages of other great civilizations, Sanskrit, Persian and Arabic, and translated texts such as the *Bhagavad Gita* into English. Their scholarship launched what Raymond Schwab called an "oriental renaissance"[28] in Europe and influenced such American literary and philosophical luminaries as Thoreau, Emerson and Whitman.

In "Living With Difference in India" we again challenged Orientalism's epistemological claim that knowledge necessarily follows power. Our vehicle this time was the contest between legal pluralism's recognition of differences in personal law and identity and legal universalism's demand for a uniform civil code and uniform citizenship. We showed that the discourse and practice associated with legal pluralism and legal universalism were shaped by the ideas and attitudes of actors situated in seven distinctive historical contexts,[29] not by a standard motive to serve power.

Processes of State Formation

Our engagement with state formation in India began in 1957, 28 years before "The Subcontinental Empire and the Regional Kingdom in Indian State Formation"[30] was published. As we set about creating a reading list and a course outline for our first course on Indian government and politics, we confronted the absence of historical and comparative analysis or theoretical writing about state formation in Asia in general and India in particular. In our education as post-graduate students interested in comparative politics, scholarship on the state in Europe and America was readily available. There was nothing equivalent for Asia, no conventional wisdom elegantly summed up in definitive textbooks such as Carl J. Friedrich's *Constitutional Government and Democracy* or Herman Finer's *The Theory and Practice of Modern Government*. Friedrich and Finer referred to Greece and Rome, the Renaissance and the Enlightenment, to Plato and Aristotle, Machiavelli, Hobbes and Bodin, Locke and Rousseau, the Magna Carta and the Treaty of Westphalia. No such iconic references were available for studying the state in India.

In the pre-war period and for a decade afterward, the study of comparative politics was unreflexively Eurocentric. When, after decolonization, social scientists began the study of "new" and "developing" nations, modernization theory, structural functionalism and Marxism called for the obliteration of the past. Knowledge about the state in Asia, of ancient kingdoms and empires, of political thought and texts, or of colonial states was neither sought nor created. European state formation was naturalized and the modern state universalized.

What passed for knowledge about the state in Asia in European thought was associated with the concept of

"Oriental Despotism." Montesquieu echoing Aristotle held that "In Asia … there reigns a spirit of servitude which has never quitted it; and in the entire history of the continent it is impossible to find a single trait that marks a free soul; only the heroism of slavery is to be seen." Major state thinkers such as Friedrich Hegel, Adam Smith, James Mill, Karl Marx, even Max Weber, wove variations on Aristotle's and Montesquieu's theme of states based on a pervasive spirit of servitude. From Constantinople to Shanghai, state–subject relations in Asia were depicted as standing in marked contrast with the freedom and consent that were said to characterize the modern state in Europe.

Susanne Rudolph's 1987 "State Formation in Asia: Prolegomenon to a Comparative Study"[31] provides a larger comparative historical framework in which Indian state formation phenomena can be understood. It includes critiques of Oriental Despotism's doctrines of servitude and the absence in Asia of intermediate powers and land ownership. In India the space between the imperial ruler and his subjects was not empty; to the contrary, it was thickly populated with regional and lesser kings (*rajas*, *nawabs*), local chiefs (*zamindars*, *jagirdars*), and village, caste, tribe and sect councils who often resisted (*fitna*) by refusing tribute, attendance at court and taxes. And in marked contrast to sovereignty and social contract state theory in Europe, in Indian political thought the institutions of society preceded and limited state authority. The good king was enjoined to uphold self-regulating village, caste, guild and sect orders of society.

In our 1985 article "The Subcontinental Empire and the Regional Kingdom in Indian State Formation,"[32] we contrast the loosely structured, segmentary, power-sharing, multinational imperial form characteristic of Indian state formation with the centralized, monopoly sovereignty, nation state form whose story European analysts projected as the evolutionary culmination of the state formation story and that Lloyd Rudolph depicts in his 2006 article "Historicizing the Modern State."[33]

Had the Holy Roman Empire, a loose aggregation of regional kingdoms that shared sovereignty, continued as the dominant European state form after the twelfth century, European state formation might have taken a course akin to that found in Asia. With the benefit of hindsight, Joseph Strayer opined that, "By 1300 it was evident that the dominant state form in Western Europe was going to be the sovereign state."[34] Yet in the first half of the sixteenth century, the Holy Roman Emperor, Charles V, ruled most of Western Europe[35] and it was not until 1806, after Napoleon's victory over Prussia at Jena, that the Holy Roman Empire formally came to an end. Nor was it the case that sovereign states were the only state form after 1300; in the Dutch Republic, the Swiss Confederation and the German iteration of the Holy Roman Empire versions of states that shared sovereignty proved viable.[36]

The collapse of the Ottoman, Hapsburg and Tsarist empires at the end of World War I seemed to confirm that the imperial state form was an anachronism in Europe. And Selig Harrison's 1960 book, *India, the Most Dangerous Decades*,[37] suggested that India's multinational federal state, a latter-day version of subcontinental empire, would soon disintegrate into nation states, thereby confirming that the imperial state form was an anachronism in Asia, too. But at roughly the moment when Harrison was predicting the demise of India's federal state, six European countries signed the Treaty of Rome (1957) joining them in a European Community that, in 1992, became the European Union and now includes states from Eastern as well as Western Europe. Europe had returned to the shared sovereignty of the imperial state form and India's federal state, far from disintegrating, has become a model of democratic multiculturalism.

Contrary to the received wisdom, it has been the territorial sovereign nation state that has become increasingly anachronistic and the shared sovereignty of federal states and cooperative international institutions that seem more appropriate for a globalizing and localizing world. Failing and failed modern states have become more frequent and troubling. And the interdependence engendered by global processes have spawned not only cooperative international institutions but also the criminal as well as the benign non-state actors of the sort that Susanne Rudolph characterizes in her 1997 article "Religion, States, and Transnational Civil Society."[38]

Processes of Institutional Change

Our articles about institutional change span 38 years of India's tumultuous independent history, from 1964 to 2002. The first one, "Generals and Politicians in India," (1964)[39] was written in the aftermath of India's defeat in a war with China in 1962. "New Dimensions in Indian Democracy" (2002)[40] was written a decade after the momentous economic reforms launched in 1991 by Prime Minister Narasimha Rao and then Finance Minister Manmohan Singh.

India's defeat by China in 1962 raised questions about its national identity, institutional arrangements and policy priorities. The defeat had a shattering effect on India's self-conception as a peaceful and secure country, its foreign and defense policies and on its capacity to pursue planned economic development. We spoke that year with Prime Minister Jawaharlal Nehru, the discredited Defense Minister Krishna Menon, the new Defense Minister Y. B. Chavan, and the US ambassador during the war, Kenneth Galbraith. The war re-opened the question of civil–military relations. Had the Indian military invited defeat by favorites of the Congress party's leadership being promoted and given commands without regard to qualification and seniority? How and why had India been able to maintain civil control of the military when Pakistan and many other new and developing nations had turned to the military for modernization? How did the defeat affect the standing and viability of India's political leadership, in particular Prime Minister Jawaharlal Nehru and Defense Minister Krishna Menon?

We congratulated ourselves on empathetic and analytic even-handedness when our conclusions in "Generals and Politicians" were published by both Menon and Chavan, with their opposing interests and views, in their respective "house" journals.

Institutional changes also followed from the initiation of economic reforms in 1991. The reforms signaled the end of India's state-dominated economy and the beginning of a market-oriented one. These processes of change were paralleled by major changes in the balance among India's political institutions. "New Dimensions" and "Redoing the Constitutional Design: From the Interventionist to the Regulatory State"[41] examine the causes and consequences of the emergence of the Supreme Court, the Election Commission, as well as the President as effective and respected institutions, and the decline in the reputation and effectiveness of the political executive and parliament.

"The Iconization of Chandrababu: Sharing Sovereignty in India's Federal Market Economy,"[42] also published in 2001, shows how economic liberalization combined with the transformation of the party system from dominant to multi-party opened the way for India's federal states to take charge of their own economic fates. With Planning Commission public investment less available and each state increasingly a tub on its own bottom, state chief ministers were challenged to compete for domestic and foreign private investment if their states were to prosper.

In the years leading up to the publication in 1980 of "The Centrist Future of Indian Politics,"[43] scholars had heatedly debated the role of class in Indian politics. Was India like China, where Mao had found class relations in the countryside that, he argued, fueled revolutionary change? Was India like the countries of Western Europe where organized labor helped class parties to play a major role in politics and governance? Was India like the United States where, according to Alexis Tocqueville and Louis Hartz, Americans were "born free" and class consciousness and class politics were, at best, marginal?

We answered that India had a distinctive centrist dynamic. Its pluralist objective conditions were inhospitable to class politics. Its indigenous categories were more often those of caste, ethnicity and religious community than they were of class. Its industrial work force was proportionately small—in 1976 its five million factory workers

constituted only 3 percent of its total work force of 180
million. The 67 percent of the work force in the agrarian sector lacked consciousness and organization. There
was hardly a shadow of a peasant–worker alliance. And
India's financial and industrial capitalist class was over-
shadowed by state firms and rendered dependent by state
regulation—the notorious "permit license raj." We offered
reasons for centrist politics to be and to remain for the
foreseeable future dominant in Indian politics, one of
which was the marginality of class politics and another the
electoral strength of upwardly mobile lower castes seeking
status and benefits.

In our 1981 article "Judicial Review versus Parliamentary
Sovereignty: The Struggle Over Stateness in India,"[44] we
addressed a central arena for institutional change, the
relative standing of parliamentary sovereignty and judicial
review in India's constitutional order. Was Parliament's
power to legislate, including its power to amend the
Constitution, unlimited as Nehruvians tended to believe,
or did the Supreme Court's power of judicial review allow
it to set limits on Parliament's power to legislate? In 1973
in *Keshavananda Bharati vs. State of Kerala*, the Court ruled
that Parliament's power to legislate and amend is not the
power to destroy. Parliamentary sovereignty is limited by
the Constitution's "basic structure" or "essential features,"
terms it was in the Court's provenance to specify, define
and apply.

"Rethinking Secularism: Genesis and Implications of the Textbook Controversy, 1977–1979"[45] examined one of the most important arenas for defining who and what is Indian, the textbooks assigned in India's schools. The most influential textbooks are written by scholars commissioned by the National Council for Educational Research and Training (NCERT). Soon after Morarji Desai's Janata-led government assumed office in 1977, questions were raised about four textbooks. It was alleged that their "controversial and biased material" would lead readers to acquire "a prejudiced view of Indian history." Written by prominent historians from a Nehruvian secular perspective, the books inter alia critiqued "communal" history, i.e. history that depicted India's Muslim minority as foreigners and interlopers in a Hindu nation.

The Desai-Jan Sangh sections of the Janata party did not take kindly to such views and moved to remove and replace the books at issue. The textbook controversy that followed renewed a century-old effort to articulate a national identity and public philosophy for India that came to grips with the role of Muslims in Indian history. The controversy anticipated the even more acrimonious and extended one that accompanied the rise in the 1990s of the BJP as a national and governing party committed to defining India as a "Hindu nation."

Our conception of institutional change encompasses non-state actors in civil society. Our 1986 article introduced a distinctive form of political representation, what we called the "demand group." Unlike interest groups which feature formal organization and continuity and operate for the most part in the corridors of power, demand groups are a more spontaneous and less formed version of collective action akin to movement and issue politics that operate "out of doors" in the public square. Their tactics and style draw on the political theater of Gandhi's non-violent non-cooperation and civil disobedience campaigns. Demand groups' natural habitats are the agrarian producers of India's vast unorganized economy and the lower castes of India's hierarchical social order.

Identity Politics

Unlike the interest group and class politics that, until recently, have been the mainstay of British and American political science, identity politics fairly quickly emerged in the study of Indian politics as a dominant category.[47] Two of our five articles on Identity Politics are about caste and one each about cultural nationalism, region and students. An early entry in the study of identity politics in India was our 1960 article "The Political Role of India's Caste Associations,"[48] an interpretation that Lloyd Rudolph elaborated in his 1965 article "The Democratic Incarnation of Caste in India."[49]

The caste association was the means by which we illustrated and supported our most significant theoretical contribution, "the modernity of tradition;" change could and did come about by adaptation of traditional institutions to new circumstances and demands.

The interpretation we gave to caste was in conflict with common political discourse in both India and the United States. Caste was not, like interest group or class, an established category in the political science canon. And caste was anathema to the modernists of the Nehruvian nationalist generation. Like those who made the French revolution, Nehruvians imagined a nation of equal citizens. For the French this entailed eradicating the institutions of the old regime, the monarchy, the aristocracy and the church; for Nehruvian nationalists it meant eradicating ascribed differences, pre-eminently caste and the caste system. Absent eradication, denial stepped in. Our early writing about caste was treated as a non-subject, an illegitimate subject or a reactionary subject.

But how was it that we came to study caste and politics? One reason was our interest in Alexis de Tocqueville. His *Democracy in America* taught that associational life was a necessary condition for democracy. So we came to India with the question of associational life on our minds. We also came with a commitment to political ethnography, e.g. finding out how those Indians living in the *mofussil*[50] and in villages as well as those living in cities who

were English educated think about self-help and collective 139
action. We tried to avoid "the imperialism of categories,"[51]
the imposition of concepts derived from European and
American experience on distant cultures and peoples.
We listened for and investigated categories used by local
actors, Vanniyars and Nadars in Madras, Jats and Rajputs
in Rajasthan. They and other groups like them practiced
self-help and collective action in what we came to call
caste associations, intentional associations that were partly
ascriptive, partly voluntary.

Studying caste associations historically and contem-
poraneously, we came upon two of India's greatest para-
doxes, that caste was anti-caste and that caste strengthened
democracy. Universal suffrage made it possible for India's
more numerous lower castes acting through caste associations to acquire political power and to use it to dismantle
the *varna* status order based on purity and pollution and
to gain respect, and benefits.

We recognize that the history of caste politics in India
is not linear. An institution that came to serve democracy
at one moment in history may fall victim to narrow parochialism at another.

Cultural identity in India is expressed in a variety
of ways, not least through the politics of its distinctive
regions. Lloyd Rudolph's 1961 article "Dravidian Politics
in Madras" and the jointly authored 1969 "Rimland and
Heartland in Indian Education"[52] captured the impor-

tance of regional differences for Indian politics, the first by analyzing the rise of cultural nationalism in today's Tamil Nadu, the second by analyzing the regional disparities that increasingly challenge the equilibrium of India's federal system.

Finally, our 1971 article on "Student Politics and National Politics in India"[53] showed how and why in the 1960s students more than workers shaped the national policy agenda.

Interpreting Lives: Amar Singh and Gandhi

In "Interpreting Lives" we turn to what has proved to be a central concern in the more recent part of our scholarly careers, the subjective knowledge available from first-person narratives such as an autobiography or a diary. We address the epistemological standing of subjective knowledge in relation to other ways of knowing and other forms of knowledge in "Engaging Subjective Knowledge."[54]

The two persons with whose first person narratives we have spent a great deal of time are Mohandas Gandhi, usually referred to as Mahatma (Great Soul) Gandhi, probably India's best known personality, and Amar Singh, a Rajput nobleman and Edwardian gentlemen whose place in history will be wrought more by his diary than by his military career in British and princely India.

Gandhi wrote an autobiography, the well known *Story of My Experiments With Truth*, the less well known autobiographical account of his 21 years in South Africa, *Satyagraha in South Africa*, and an enormous number of letters, most of which have been made available in the 100 volumes of his collected works. Amar Singh wrote extended reflexive accounts every day for 44 years, from September 1898 when he was 19 to November 1942 when he died at the age of 64. The manuscript diary is bound in 89 volumes of about 800 pages each. It may be the world's longest continuous diary.[55]

Our engagement with Gandhi goes back to the mid-1950s when we first approached the study of Indian politics. The memory of Gandhi was still vivid in the West and in India. Courses on Indian politics or history assigned Nehru's *The Discovery of India* and Gandhi's *The Story of My Experiments With Truth*.[56] We had to work out an interpretation. Susanne Rudolph published two articles on Gandhi in *World Politics* in the early 1960s, "The New Courage" and "Conflict and Consensus in Indian Politics." Their titles convey the gist of their arguments.[57] We never got tired of Gandhi and kept thinking and writing about him.[58] As independence drew near Nehru and other high modernists marginalized his ideas, dismissing his 1909 critique of modern civilization in *Hind Swaraj* as "completely unreal."[59] In the 1990s Lloyd Rudolph taught a course on Gandhi at the University of Chicago and our most recent book about him, *Postmodern Gandhi and Other Essays: Gandhi in the World and at Home*, was published in India and the US in 2006.[60]

Our work on Amar Singh arose from our involvement with Rajasthan. It began in 1956 when we arrived in Jaipur, the state's capital, after our overland trip from London in a Land Rover. We returned ten times on research trips. Since "retiring" in 2002 we spend January through March in Jaipur writing and enjoying our friends and the Jaipur festival.

The kingdoms of Rajasthan, Jaipur, Jodhpur, Udaipur, Bikaner and others, had been part of princely India, the two-fifths of the subcontinent that Britain ruled indirectly. That indirectness, in our view, sheltered Rajasthan from some of the effects of colonial modernity, enabling those living there to retain more of their way of life. Rajasthanis had less of a colonial consciousness.

In "Becoming a Diarist: Amar Singh's Construction of an Indian Personal Document" (1988)[61] we unpack the apparent anomaly of why and how a Hindi-speaking Rajput Thakur wrote a diary in English over 44 years. He says the diary became "his best friend," gave him refuge from the philistinism and boredom of his raj and Rajput colleagues and kept him amused.

We first encountered the diary in 1971 when Colonel Kesri Singh, Amar Singh's debonair and literary younger brother, introduced us to Amar Singh's nephew. Mohan Singh was Amar Singh's heir and as such the guardian and early interpreter of the diary. We took to him and he took to us. For 30 years off and on we worked together on selecting, editing and interpreting the diary. In 2000 we and Mohan Singh published *Reversing the Gaze*,[62] a title that draws attention to a 'native' constructing the colonial other. Most of the 625-page book is based on 1 percent of the diary's first seven years.

There is a special kind of truth about Amar Singh's daily reflections; he does not know how things will turn out so he cannot retrospectively rationalize what he has said and done. At the same time his daily accounts and occasional essays are remarkably reflexive, partly a result, we believe, of the dual sensibility that his liminal positioning between princely and British India engenders.

Amar Singh can be an ethnographer of Rajput and raj culture because his reflexivity enables him, in T. N. Madan's phrase, to render the familiar unfamiliar. By treating culture as contested as well as prescriptive, he can tell us about culture in the making as well as in the doing. We see this capacity illustrated in "Setting the Table: Amar Singh on the *S. S. Mohawk*."[63] And in "Self as Other" (1997)[64] we show how Amar Singh, because he is, in his own person, observer, informant, narrator and author, can practice what we call "self as other" ethnography.

Throughout our careers as scholars of India we have been concerned with India's relationships with its regional neighbors, not least Pakistan, with how US policy impacts the South Asia region, and with bilateral relations between India and the US. Our concerns have occasionally gone beyond the academic; from time to time we have advised US administrations, the latest being the Clinton administration, and briefed newly appointed US ambassadors to India. But our main concern with foreign policy has been academic. It is reflected in a number of papers written between 1983, when Cold War bipolarity made it possible for India to practice non-alignment, and 2008, when India had to make its way in a world where a unilateralist US was the only superpower.[65]

"The United States, India and South Asia" (1983)[66] distinguishes the South Asian region from the other four developing country regions, the Middle East, Latin America, Southeast Asia, and Africa. India, by six "power" variables, surpasses her neighbors more decisively than any one power does its neighbors in the other regions. It is, in that sense, the "natural" hegemon.[67] The article shows that India's proportion of the regional totals for each of the six variables averages about two-thirds while in the other four regions the largest country (Egypt, Brazil,

Indonesia, and Nigeria) averages about one-third of the total for the region. Yet India has not been able to exercise the regional hegemony that its power should make possible.[68] Rather, the South Asia region has experienced four wars between India and Pakistan since independence and partition in 1947. Why?

We address the causes of regional instability in South Asia in "The Making of U.S. Foreign Policy For South Asia: Offshore Balancing in Historical Perspective" (2006).[69] There we argue that during the Cold War, including the 10 years (1979–89) that the Soviets fought to hold Afghanistan, the US unduly subordinated its interest in South Asia regional stability to its containment policy against the Soviet Union. From the early days of CENTO and SEATO in the mid-1950s, the US used Pakistan to practice "offshore balancing,"[70] a policy that enabled Pakistan to challenge India in South Asia.

"The Great Game in Asia: Revisited and Revised" (1985) invoked Kipling's metaphor of the "great game" to analyze the Soviet effort in 1979 to extend its power over Afghanistan.[71] The article anticipated a return in scholarly and policy analysis to the metaphor of the great game that Kipling, in his masterful novel *Kim* used to characterize the contest for mastery in Central Asia between the Tsarist and British empires. By 1989 the Soviets had experienced the failure that the British experienced in 1842 and 1880 when they tried to establish their authority in Afghanistan, an experience that may beset US efforts post-9/11 to establish a friendly regime there.

"The Faltering Novitiate: Rajiv at Home and Abroad in 1988" examines the interaction of foreign and domestic politics during Rajiv Gandhi's term as prime minister.[72] Unlike much of the foreign policy or international relations literature, it does not treat the state as a "black box" or a unified national actor. Foreign policy failures, e.g. the Rajiv Gandhi-initiated intervention on behalf of the LTTE (Liberation Tigers of Tamil Eelam) in Sri Lanka's civil war, diminished his standing in domestic politics. More serious still was the Bofors gun kickback scandal that sufficiently tarnished his and the party's image that they were driven from office in the 1989 election.

Rajiv Gandhi's government began with an unprecedented mandate from the 1984 election. Led by "Mr. Clean," the handsome, youthful son of the martyred Indira Gandhi, Congress won a higher percentage of votes, 49 percent, and seats, 71 percent, than in any election before or since. Rajiv Gandhi seemed poised to move India into the twenty-first century, to introduce honesty, technological change and political and economic reform, and to raise India's standing in the region and the world. Relations with the US improved greatly; the warmth with which his address in June 1985 to a joint session of the US

Congress was received was a measure both of its quality 147
and of India's new standing in America's eyes.

But by mid-term his leadership and government
began to falter. His effort to end the "permit license raj"
lost momentum and to reform a corrupt and undemo-
cratic Congress party was stillborn. When he tried to turn
India into a major power by spending more for two years
on arms purchases than any other country, he dangerously escalated Indian debt and precipitated the Bofors
gun kickback scandal. His effort to patronize and tame the
LTTE leader P. Prabhakaran by having India intervene as
a peacekeeper in Sri Lanka's violent secessionist struggle
soon proved an embarrassing and costly failure. At the
next election in 1989 Congress lost in large part because
Rajiv Gandhi had become a political liability.

Susanne Rudolph's 1997 essay "Dehomogenizing
Religious Formations; An Alternative to the Clash of
Civilizations Thesis" arose out of a US Social Science
Research Council study group related to its program on
International Peace and Security.[73] It was created in
the early 1990s to consider alternatives to the standard
international relations view of security, that it was defined
by and limited to state actors and that their power was
defined primarily in military terms. Rudolph's essay questions whether the state can continue to be considered a
reliable unit for the study of international relations when

WRITING INDIA

sovereign boundaries have lost legitimacy and effectiveness. It expands the study of security to include the actors that constitute transnational civil society. In an era of fading states and fading ideologies, religious actors and religious narratives have assumed more prominence.

The world began to pay attention to the role of religion in defining security when in 1979 a radical Islamic regime displaced the Shah of Iran and the Soviets entered the Afghanistan quagmire. Susanne Rudolph's 1997 essay became an early response to Samuel Huntington's provocative thesis, first stated in his 1993 *Foreign Affairs* article, that the world was witnessing a "Clash of Civilizations."[74] The ideological and geopolitical divisions of the cold war would be succeeded by civilizational differences that could pit "The West against the Rest." Civilizations for Huntington were defined by a number of elements such as language and culture but by far the most important defining element was religion.

Huntington treated civilizations and civilizational states as homogenous unified actors in international relations. Rudolph took issue with Huntington's deterministic primordialism. Civilizations, religions and states, she argued, are heterogeneous. Christians, Muslims and Hindus come in many variations; they vary with place, time and context. Identity, meaning and policy are contested and constructed, products of internal and external processes of debate and interaction. Even as US policy makers during the 1960s had mistakenly persuaded themselves that Communist regimes had a common interest that overrode the power of nationalism, there is a danger in the millennium that the Huntington perspective on religion will produce a similar reductionist view.

Writing as Public Intellectuals

Our writing as public intellectuals can be distinguished from our more strictly academic writing by the nature of the readers to whom it is addressed. Colleagues in the academy, fellow professionals, are one kind of public. Colleagues in the public sphere, those concerned with ideas and policy, are another kind of public. This raises the question of what voices we have used over the years. We have spent enough time in India—a total of 12 research years—that we have had to address our work to two audiences, each of which brings very different orientations and backgrounds to the table. For example, US students in the 1960s who doubted that a poor country could be democratic or that a multi-linguistic, multicultural country could cohere as a nation required different answers than Delhi-located faculty colleagues. The positive voice we adopted to persuade US public opinion that both democracy and multiculturalism were reasonably compatible in India seemed excessively sanguine to our critically minded Indian colleagues.

Our essays as public intellectuals were written to influence thought and opinion in the American public sphere.
Over the years, we have tried to keep up something of a
public presence back home in America for our work on
India.

The intelligent reader had many questions: As the
1950s gave way to the 1960s we like other India-*wallahs*
were asked, "After Nehru Who?" The first essay in this
section, "India Turns to a Conciliator," was published in
the *New York Times Magazine* of June 14, 1964, two weeks
after Nehru's death on May 27, 1964. It addressed that
question by introducing *New York Times* readers to Lal
Bahadur Shastri and, perhaps equally important, to the
Congress party's heroic history as a nationalist movement
and as an effectively functioning political party.

Other questions often asked by intelligent lay readers
about India are, "how can so diverse a country survive
as a nation?" and "how can democracy thrive when literacy is so low?" Some of the articles address these kinds
of questions. The first to do so is an article published on
the eve of the 1967 election, "India Campaigns: Cows,
Corruption and Demonstrations."[75] Thousands of sadhus
were camped on Delhi's ring road and some of them had
"stormed" Parliament. An early manifestation of Hindu
politics, they signaled Congress' weakening hold in
Northern India and were a harbinger of its near loss of the

fourth parliamentary election. A 1993 article, "Modern Hate: How Ancient Animosities Get Invented,"[76] criticized President's Clinton's use of the term "primordial" in the context of the unfolding ethnic violence in the former Yugoslavia. It used evidence from India to argue that ethnic differences were politically constructed, not primordial, and that living with ethnic differences was not only possible but also could be desirable as a form of pluralism that supported democracy. Published in a 1993 number of *The New Republic*, a widely circulated journal of opinion, the article had considerable impact in political and policy circles and was used in college and university courses. It also influenced methodological debates in the academy by pitting constructivism against essentialism in explaining difference and identity.

"Organized Chaos: Why India Works,"[77] published five years later in 1998, asked, "How can a land of six major religions, 18 official languages, and 3,500 subcastes be a democracy that works? How has India managed to defy the post–Cold War conventional wisdom that multinational states are subject to ethnic violence and civil war?" After analyzing the turbulent politics associated with the rise of Hindu nationalism and OBC reservations, the article argued that "fifty years after independence, this pluralist system remains alive and well. It has weathered the challenges from Hindu nationalism, been revitalized by protracted social revolution, and been sustained by a culturally diverse federal system and a pluralist state that knows how to share sovereignty."

Five articles explored India's identity and culture. Susanne Rudolph's "From Madras: A View of the Southern Film" (1971)[78] uses Shivaji Ganesan's life and film career to characterize his contribution to the Southern film industry and to politics in Madras. In "Jaipur Notes: Experiencing the Emergency" (1977)[79] we recount how we, our children and a young German au pair experienced encounters with the Emergency while living in Jaipur in 1975–76.

In "The East Psychoanalyzed" (1986)[80] Lloyd Rudolph intervened in a debate about whether, as Lucian Pye argued in *Asian Power and Politics: The Cultural Dimensions of Authority*,[81] Asian politics were different than US and European. For Pye, Asians and Indians as well as Chinese, Japanese and others, were products of a psycho-cultural version of what Montesquieu called Asian despotism: "In Asia," Montesquieu argued, and as stated earlier, "there reigns a spirit of servitude which has never quitted it; and in the entire history of the continent it is impossible to find a single trait that marks a free soul; only the heroism of slavery is to be seen."[82] According to Pye, "When Asians say how much they revere their fathers, they are really saying how much they fear them. When on occasion they give vent to anger at surrogate authority figures and become consumed with hatred, they are at last expressing what has been repressed."[83] Lloyd Rudolph asks, "Does the Oedipal rage really explain the Taiping rebellion or Gandhian nationalism?"

Susanne Rudolph's "All the Raj in Jaipur"[84] examines how polo was transformed from the sport of kings to the sport of the middle classes and the tourists. First jewelers, then banks, breweries and telecom firms joined the royals and the Army as patrons of the game. Jaipur's polo season has helped to make Jaipur into "destination city."

Finally, Lloyd Rudolph in "The Occidental Tagore" challenges Martha Nussbaum's effort to use Rabindranath Tagore's novel *The Home and the World* to make a moral case for a universal human nature and the naturalness of world citizenship.[85] In her 1994 essay "Patriotism and Cosmopolitanism," Nussbaum revives the notion of a generalized "human sensibility" that makes it possible to translate all cultures into one another's terms. In doing so she invokes the Tagore who is a "world poet," and an apostle of world citizenship. Lloyd Rudolph argues that Nussbaum's universal subverts the local. The Bengali Tagore whose poetry conveys "some of the most striking records of the details of Bengali life ever written," he suggests, is subverted by a Tagore who "orientalized and exoticized his translations from his own work to suit Western taste."

What took us to India in 1956 was its location on a new frontier, post-colonial government and politics. The study of "new nations" offered a fresh landscape for the study of comparative politics, an alternative to studying the "old" political science of Europe and America. The problems were new. The professional journals had yet to address them. Now India has become an "Asian tiger," candidate for superpower status, a high-growth economy, its business magnates competing with Europeans for status, its depressed lower castes on the march when not already in charge, its practice of democracy habitual if not always clean or effective. Sixty-one years after independence it is no longer a "new nation."

Notes and References

1. We have been asked by the Editors of *India Review* "to reflect upon how both India and our field of study [Political Science] have evolved over the course of our careers." We have drawn on the introductory essays in our recent three-volume work, *Explaining Indian Democracy: A Fifty Year Perspective* (New Delhi: Oxford University Press, 2008). I. *The Realm of Ideas: Inquiry and Theory*; II. *The Realm of Institutions: State Formation and Institutional Change*; III. *The Realm of the Public Sphere: Identity and Policy*.

2. Chicago: University of Chicago Press, 1967.

3. See S. M. Lipset, "Some Social Requisites of Democracy: Economic Development and Political Legitimacy," *American Political Science Review* Vol. 53 (March 1959), pp. 61–105, for the hypothesis and supporting evidence that democracy should be an utter failure in India.

4. For the dichotomous "pattern variables" see Talcott Parsons and Edward Shils, "Categories of the Orientation and Organization of Action," in Talcott Parsons and Edward Shils, eds., *Toward a General Theory of Action* (Cambridge, MA: Harvard University Press, 1951). The variables are: 1. Affectivity–Affective Neutrality; 2. Self-orientation–Collectivity-orientation; 3. Universalism–Particularism; 4. Ascription–Achievement; 5. Specificity–Diffuseness (p. 77).

5. In "A Functional Approach to Comparative Politics" which introduced Gabriel Almond and James S. Coleman, eds., *The Politics of the Developing Areas* (Princeton: Princeton University Press, 1960), the first of seven volumes on "Studies in Political Development" sponsored by the Committee on Comparative Politics of the Social Science Research Council, Gabriel Almond wrote "the concept of political system [serves] … to separate out analytically the structures which perform functions in all societies regardless of scale of differentiation, and culture." Those functions are divided into "input functions," i.e. 1. political socialization and recruitment; 2. interest articulation; 3. interest aggregation; 4. political communication; and "output functions," i.e. 5. rule-making; 6. rule application; and 7. rule adjudication. The essay is reproduced in Gabriel Almond, *Political Development: Essays in Heuristic Theory* (Boston: Little Brown and Company, 1970), pp. 79–151. The quote is from pp. 81–2 and the input and output functions are at p. 96.

6. For a recent critical but positive evaluation of area studies see David Szanton's essay "Introduction: The Origin, Nature and Challenges of Area Studies in the United States," in David Szanton, ed., *The Politics of Knowledge: Area Studies and the Disciplines* (Berkeley and Los Angeles: University of California Press, 2004), pp. 1–33.

7. See Susanne Hoeber Rudolph's APSA Presidential address, "The Imperialism of Categories: Situating Knowledge in a Globalizing World," *Perspectives on Politics* Vol. 3, No. 5 (March 2005), pp. 5–14, for an elaboration of the concept of "situated knowledge."

8. Several of our books are about Rajasthan. We have helped to organize five international conferences on Rajasthan and a Rajasthan Studies Group list-serve and participated in the publication of six composite books on what might be called Rajasthan studies. Among these are Susanne Hoeber Rudolph and Lloyd I. Rudolph, *Reversing the Gaze: A Colonial Subject's Narrative of Imperial India* (New Delhi: Oxford University Press, 2002); Susanne Hoeber Rudolph and Lloyd I. Rudolph, *Essays on Rajputana* (New Delhi: Concept, 1984); and Karine Schomer, Joan Erdman, Deryck O. Lodrick, and Lloyd I. Rudolph, *The Idea of Rajasthan: Explorations in Regional Identity* (New Delhi: Manohar, 1994).

9. Kristen Renwick Monroe, ed., *Perestroika! The Raucous Revolution in Political Science* (New Haven, CT: Yale University Press, 2005).

10. "Surveys in India: Field Experience in Madras State," *Public Opinion Quarterly* Vol. 22, No. 3 (1958), pp. 235–44.

11. "Determinants and Varieties of Agrarian Mobilization," in Meghnad Desai, Susanne Hoeber Rudolph, and Ashok Rudra,

eds., *Agrarian Power and Agricultural Productivity in South Asia* (Berkeley: University of California Press, 1984).

12. Ours may have been the first random sample survey in India. (Eric De Costa's surveys emphasized urban responses.) Its protocols are on deposit with the archive established by Yogendra Yadav at the Centre for the Study of Developing Societies in Delhi.

13. "Engaging Subjective Knowledge: How Amar Singh's Diary Narratives of and by the Self Explain Identity Formation," *Perspectives on Politics* Vol. 1, No. 4 (December 2003), pp. 681–94; "The Imperialism of Categories: Situating Knowledge in a Globalizing World," *Perspectives on Politics* Vol. 3, No. 5 (March 2005), pp. 5–14; "Perestroika and Its Other," in Monroe, ed., *Perestroika!* pp. 12–20; "Let a Hundred Flowers Bloom, Let a Hundred Thoughts Contend," in Monroe, ed., *Perestroika!* pp. 230–6.

14. "Reconnecting Theory and History: Or Moving Beyond Fordist Political Science," *Clio: Newsletter of Politics & History* Vol. 17, No. 1 (Fall/Winter 2006–7), pp. 1 and 53.

15. *World Politics* Vol. 13, No. 3 (April 1961), pp. 355–99.

16. See W. H. Morris-Jones, *Government and Politics in India* (London: Hutchinson University Library, 1964), pp. 52–61, where he spoke of the "languages of Indian politics, the modern, the traditional and the saintly," and Myron Weiner, "Struggle Against Power: Notes on Indian Political Behavior," *World Politics* Vol. 8, No. 3 (April 1956), p. 395, where he spoke of how the "traditional attitudes which affect current political behavior" affect "the prospects for success of Indian democratic institutions."

17. Chicago: University of Chicago Press, 1967, pp. 3–14.

18. "Authority and Power in Bureaucratic and Patrimonial Administration: A Revisionist Interpretation of Weber on Bureaucracy," *World Politics* Vol. 31, No. 2 (January 1979), pp. 195–227.

19. *Economic and Political Weekly* Vol. 35, No. 2 (May 2000), pp. 1762–99.

20. Niraja Gopal Jayal, Sudha Pai and Vishnu Mohapatra were conducting field work projects in UP and Orissa in collaboration with the University of Uppsala.

21. Lloyd I. Rudolph, "The Media and Cultural Politics," *Economic and Political Weekly* Vol. 27, No. 28 (June 1992), pp. 159–79.

22. Lloyd I. Rudolph and Susanne Hoeber Rudolph, "Occidentalism and Orientalism: Perspectives on Legal Pluralism," in Sally Humphreys, ed., *Cultures of Scholarship* (Ann Arbor: University of Michigan Press, 1997), pp. 219–51.

23. Susanne Hoeber Rudolph and Lloyd I. Rudolph, "Living with Difference in India: Legal Pluralism and Legal Universalism in Historical Context," in Gerald James Larson, ed., *Religion and Personal Law in Secular India: A Call to Judgment* (Bloomington, IN: Indiana University Press, 2001).

24. New York: Pantheon, 1978.

25. Rosane Rocher begins her "British Orientalism in the 18th Century: The Dialectic of Knowledge and Government," in Carol A. Breckenridge and Peter van der Veer, eds., *Orientalism and the Postcolonial Predicament* (Philadelphia: University of Pennsylvania Press, 1993) by finding that Edward Said's critique "does to orientalist scholarship what it accuses orientalist scholarship of having done to the countries east of Europe; it creates a single discourse, undifferentiated by space and time and cross political, social, and intellectual identities," p. 215.

26. William Jones, "A Discourse on the Institution of a Society for Enquiring into the History, Civil and Natural, the Antiquities, Arts, Sciences, and Literature of Asia," *Asiatic Researches* Vol. I (1806), pp. ix–x.

27. See Om Prakash Kejariwal, *The Asiatic Society of Bengal and the Discovery of India's Past, 1784–1838* (Delhi and New York: Oxford University Press, 1988).

28. See Raymond Schwab, *The Oriental Renaissance; Europe's Rediscovery of India and the East, 1680–1880* (New York: Columbia University Press, 1984).

29. Those contexts were: 1. the East India Company eras of Warren Hastings and the scholars of the Asiatic Society of Bengal and of William Bentinck and the Utilitarians and Evangelicals; 2. the trauma of the 1857 rebellion and its aftermath, Queen Victoria's 1858 Proclamation accepting difference; 3. the fracture of partition as it was foreshadowed in Sir Sayyad Ahmed Khan's "many nations" doctrine; 4. Mohammed Ali Jinnah's two nation doctrine; 5. the Indian National Congress' universalist one nation, equal citizenship doctrine; 6. the cohabitation in Congress' secularism doctrine between equal recognition of all religions and special privileging of minority religion, particularly Islam; and 7. the rise of the Hindu nationalist ideology in the 1980s and the BJP universalist doctrine of an homogenous Hindu nation.

30. Lloyd I. Rudolph and Susanne Hoeber Rudolph, "The Subcontinental Empire and the Regional Kingdom in Indian State Formation," in Paul Wallace, ed., *Region and Nation in India* (New Delhi: Oxford and IVH Publishing Company, 1985), pp. 40–59.

31. Susanne Hoeber Rudolph, "Presidential Address: State Formation in Asia—Prolegomenon to a Comparative Study,"

160   *The Journal of Asian Studies* Vol. XLVI, No. 4 (November 1987), pp. 731–45.

32. Paul Wallace, *Region and Nation in India* (New Delhi: Oxford and IBH, 1985).

33. Lloyd I. Rudolph and John Kurt Jacobsen, "Historicizing the Modern State," in Lloyd I. Rudolph and John Kurt Jacobsen, eds., *Experiencing the State* (New Delhi and New York: Oxford University Press, 2006), pp. vii–xxix.

34. Joseph Strayer, *On the Medieval Origins of the Modern State* (Princeton, NJ: Princeton University Press, 1970), p. 10.

35. The Hapsburg Charles V was Holy Roman Emperor from 1519 to 1556. Concurrently he was ruler of Burgundian Netherlands, King of Aragon, King of Castile, King of Naples and Sicily, and Archduke of Austria.

36. See Dimitrios Karmis and Wayne Norman, eds., *Theories of Federalism: A Reader* (New York: Palgrave Macmillan, 2005), and Joon Suk Kim, "Making States Federatively: Different Routes of State Formation in Late Medieval and Early Modern Europe," PhD, Department of Political Science, University of Chicago, 2004.

37. Selig Harrison, *India, the Most Dangerous Decade* (Princeton, NJ: Princeton University Press, 1960).

38. Susanne Hoeber Rudolph, "Religion, States and Transnational Civil Society," in Susanne Hoeber Rudolph and James Piscatori, eds., *Transnational Religion and Fading States* (Boulder, CO: Westview Press, 1997), pp. 1–24.

39. Lloyd I. Rudolph and Susanne Hoeber Rudolph, "Generals and Politicians in India," *Pacific Affairs* Vol. XXXVII, No. 6 (Spring 1964), pp. 15–37.

40. Susanne Hoeber Rudolph and Lloyd I. Rudolph, "New

Dimensions of Indian Democracy," *Journal of Democracy* Vol.
13, No. 1 (January 2002), pp. 52–66.

41. Lloyd I. Rudolph and Susanne Hoeber Rudolph, "Redoing the Constitutional Design: From an Interventionist to a Regulatory State," in Atul Kohli, ed., *The Success of India's Democracy* (Cambridge: Cambridge University Press, 2001), pp. 127–62.

42. Lloyd I. Rudolph and Susanne Hoeber Rudolph, "The Iconization of Chandrababu Naidu: Sharing Sovereignty in India's Federal Market Economy," *Economic and Political Weekly* Vol. 36, No. 18 (May 5, 2001), pp. 1541–52.

43. Susanne Hoeber Rudolph and Lloyd I. Rudolph, "The Centrist Future of Indian Politics," *Asian Survey* Vol. XX, No. 6 (June 1980), pp. 575–94.

44. Lloyd I. Rudolph and Susanne Hoeber Rudolph, "Judicial Review *versus* Parliamentary Sovereignty: The Struggle over Stateness in India," *Journal of Commonwealth and Comparative Politics* Vol. XIX, No. 3 (November 1981), pp. 231–56.

45. Lloyd I. Rudolph and Susanne Hoeber Rudolph, "Rethinking Secularism: Genesis and Implications of the Textbook Controversy, 1977–79," *Pacific Affairs* Vol. 56, No. 6 (Spring 1983), pp. 15–37.

46. Lloyd I. Rudolph and Susanne Hoeber Rudolph, "Demand Groups and Pluralist Representation in India," *Journal of Commonwealth and Comparative Politics* Vol. XXIV, No. 3 (November 1986), pp. 227–38.

47. With the emergence in the 1960s of feminist theory, the civil rights movement and third-world immigration, gender, race, ethnic and minority politics became the basis for American versions of identity politics.

48. *Pacific Affairs* Vol. 33, No. 1 (March 1960), pp. 5–22.

49. "The Modernity of Tradition: The Democratic Incarnation of Caste in India," *The American Political Science Review* Vol. 59, No. 1 (December 1965), pp. 975–89.

50. "The country stations and districts, as contra-distinguished from 'the Presidency'," Henry Yule and A. C. Burnell, *Hobson-Jobson: A Glossary of Anglo-Indian Colloquial Words and Phrases* (New Delhi: Munshiram Manoharlal, 1994), p. 570.

51. "The imperialism of categories" is a phrase we first used in the Introduction of *The Modernity of Tradition* (1967). Susanne Rudolph used "the imperialism of categories" as the title of her American Political Science Association Presidential address.

52. "Urban Life and Populist Radicalism: Dravidian Politics in Madras," *The Journal of Asian Studies* Vol. 20, No. 3 (May 1961), pp. 283–97; "Regional Patterns of Education: Rimland and Heartland in Indian Education," *Economic and Political Weekly* Vol. 4, No. 26 (June 28, 1969), pp. 1039–49.

53. "Student Politics and National Politics in India," *Economic and Political Weekly* Vol. 6, No. 31 (July 31, 1971), pp. 1655–68.

54. "Engaging Subjective Knowledge: How Amar Singh's Diary Narratives of and by the Self Explain Identity Formation," *Perspectives on Politics* Vol. 1, No. 4 (December 2003), pp. 681–94.

55. Mohandas K. Gandhi, *An Autobiography: The Story of My Experiments With Truth* (Boston: Beacon, 1993); Mohandas K. Gandhi, *Satyagraha in South Africa* (Ahmedabad: Navajivan, 1929); Amar Singh, *Reversing the Gaze: The Amar Singh Diary, A Colonial Subject's Narrative of Imperial India* (Boulder, CO: Westview Press, 2002).

56. Jawaharlal Nehru, *The Discovery of India* (New York: John Day, 1946).

57. *World Politics* Vol. 13, No. 3 (April 1961), pp. 385–99 and Vol. 16, No. 1 (October 1963), pp. 98–119.

58. In 1967 we carried the process forward in Part II of *The Modernity of Tradition* (Chicago: University of Chicago Press), and in 1983 we published *Gandhi: The Traditional Roots of Charisma* separately as a book (Chicago: University of Chicago Press).

59. Mohandas K. Ghandi, in Anthony J. Parel, ed., *Hind Swaraj* (Cambridge: Cambridge University Press, 1997).

60. (Chicago: University of Chicago Press).

61. *The Indian Economic and Social History Review* Vol. 25, No. 2 (1988), pp. 113–32.

62. Susanne Hoeber Rudolph and Lloyd I. Rudolph with Mohan Singh Kanota, *Reversing the Gaze: Amar Singh's Diary, A Colonial Subject's Narrative of Imperial India* (New Delhi: Oxford University Press, 2000, and Boulder CO: Westview Press, 2001).

63. Susanne Hoeber Rudolph and Lloyd I. Rudolph, "Setting the Table: Amar Singh aboard the *SS Mohawk*," *Setting the Table* Vol. 3, No. 1 (Spring 1994), pp. 158–77.

64. Lloyd I. Rudolph, "Self as Other: Amar Singh's Diary as Reflexive 'Native' Ethnography," *Modern Asian Studies* Vol. 31, No. 1 (1997), pp. 143–75.

65. We have published two books on US foreign policy toward India and Susanne Rudolph has co-edited and contributed to a book that attempts to re-orient the study of International Relations. The books about Indo-US relations are: *The Regional Imperative: The Administration of U.S. Foreign Policy Toward South Asian States Under Presidents Johnson and*

Nixon (New Delhi: Concept Publishing Company, and Atlantic Highlands, NJ: Humanities Press, 1980), e-books on India @ www.IdeaIndia.com, 2007, and *Making US Foreign Policy Toward South Asia* (New Delhi: Concept Publishing Company, 2008, and Bloomington, IN: Indiana University Press, 2008). Susanne Hoeber Rudolph and James Piscatori have co-edited *Transnational Religion and Fading States* (Boulder, CO: Westview Press, 1997).

66. In John P. Lewis and V. Kallab, eds., *US Foreign Policy and the Third World: Agenda 1983* (New York: Praeger, 1983).

67. The six "power" variables are: GNP; Population; Armed Forces; Military Expenditures; Installed Energy; and World Trade (Exports and Imports).

68. Michael C. Desch explains how US hegemony in the Americas has produced regional stability and enabled the US to become a world power in *When the Third World Matters: Latin America and the United States Grand Strategy* (Baltimore: Johns Hopkins University Press, 1993).

69. *Economic and Political Weekly* Vol. 41, No. 8 (February 25, 2006), pp. 703–9.

70. We borrow the term "offshore balancing" from Stephen Walt and John Mearsheimer but use it in the ordinary language sense of an outsider adding its weight to an indigenous regional balance. See Stephen M. Walt, *The Origin of Alliances* (Ithaca, NY: Cornell University Press, 1987) and *Taming American Power: The Global Response to US Primacy* (New York: Norton, 2005) and John J. Mearsheimer, *The Tragedy of Great Power Politics* (New York: Norton, 2001).

71. Lloyd I. Rudolph, "The Great Game in Asia: Revisited and Revised," *Crossroads: An International Socio-Political Journal* Vol. 16 (1985), pp. 1–46.

72. In Marshall L. Bouton and Philip Oldenburg, eds., *India*
Briefing, 1989 (Boulder, CO: Westview Press, 1989), pp. 1–34.

73. In Susanne Hoeber Rudolph and James Piscatori, eds., *Traditional Religion and Fading States* (Boulder, CO: Westview Press, 1997), pp. 243–61.

74. Samuel P. Huntington, "The Clash of Civilizations," *Foreign Affairs* No. 72 (Summer 1993), pp. 22–49. See also *The Clash of Civilizations and the Remaking of World Order* (New York: Simon Schuster, 1996).

75. *The Nation*, January 30, 1967, pp. 138–43.

76. *The New Republic*, March 22, 1993, pp. 24–9.

77. *The New Republic*, March 16, 1998, pp. 19–20.

78. *Yale Review*, Spring 1971, pp. 468–80.

79. *University of Chicago Magazine* (Summer 1977), pp. 9–22.

80. Lloyd I. Rudolph, "The East Psychoanalyzed," *New York Times Book Review*, February 9, 1986.

81. Lucian W. Pye and Mary W. Pye, *Asian Power and Politics: The Cultural Dimensions of Authority* (Cambridge, MA: Harvard University Press, 1986).

82. Baron de Montesquieu, *The Spirit of the Laws*, translated by Thomas Nugent (New York: Hafner, 1949), p. 269.

83. Pye, *Asian Power*, pp. 326–7.

84. *Polo* (September 1992), pp. 33–6.

85. See the *Boston Review* Vol. XIX, No. 5 (October/November, 1994), special issue for Martha Nussbaum's essay, "Patriotism or Cosmopolitanism?"

The Imperialism of
Categories
Situating Knowledge in a
Globalizing World

This is the revised version of the essay which was published in
Perspectives on Politics, vol. 3, issue 1 (March 2005),
pp. 5–14.

Category Imperialism Encountered

In February 1957 we set forth into the "heat and dust" villages of Thanjavur district, South India, with 10 Indian graduate students from Madras Christian College. Our objective was to conduct a survey on political consciousness. Six hundred urban and rural Tamils scattered across three districts constituted the random sample we had selected from the first electoral rolls of recently freed India. V. O. Key, that witty and groundbreaking doyen of electoral behavior analysis, had enticed us into survey research. Upon our return, the Michigan Survey Research Center provided a methodologically intense summer.[1]

We were part of a wave of comparativist political scientists who had been motivated in the 1950s and 1960s by the proliferation of new nations following decolonization. Gabriel Almond, a senior participant in this move, wrote that political scientists moved into Asia, the Middle East, Africa, and Latin America "with all of the energy and commitment of pioneers who wanted to be the first to observe these new experiments in politics, or to observe primordial and traditional societies with the curiosity and fascination that we associate with anthropological field work."[2]

We had tuned in early to the liberating part of survey research. Survey data freed political scientists from the formalist/legalist approaches that characterized the institutionalism of that time. Survey results told us what the citizens thought they were experiencing and doing. It gave us access to the electoral behavior and political attitudes that shaped the practical meaning of political institutions. We imagined we were plumbing the true underpinnings of the Indian experiment in democracy.

What we had not counted on was that American ideology, America's hegemonic Lockean liberalism, would shape the very concepts and methods we used to acquire knowledge about an unfamiliar society and its politics.

When our bewildered Indian interviewers returned from their first foray into the villages of Tamil Nadu, they complained of a radical disconnect between their training experience, modeled on best US practice of that time, and their field experience. The model for the performance we call an interview placed the interviewer with his clipboard in the kitchen or living room of a suburban home, where he would record the personal opinions of the housewife within—a simple two-person interaction between an interviewer and an interviewee. This model highlights the assumptions of methodological individualism that characterize survey research as practiced in the United States. Respondents are singular. They respond one on one. Not so in Tamil villages circa 1957: husbands and fathers, sons and daughters joined in. Responding to a survey question became a matter of collective deliberation, a veritable group seminar. The experience instructed us that in village India the individual was not the unit of opinion. Indeed, the singular, private, and personal were alien to the life worlds of Indian towns and villages. Opinion we learned, was collectively formed and often collectively expressed.

Survey research also operates with radically democratic assumptions: each individual's opinion and vote are assumed to have equal importance and weight. In 1957, they did not have equal weight, although in succeeding decades that difference has diminished. Our interviews were conducted at a time when caste hierarchy and patron/client relationships substantially influenced political relationships. Lower castes had not yet realized the leverage their numbers would give them in democratic elections. They soon learned to use their numerical advantage to counter the status and economic power of middle and upper castes. So the local knowledge that we then encountered, that the influence of leading landlords and caste and village headmen shaped village attitudes, opinions and votes, was not misplaced.

Our 1957 Madras survey introduced us to the problem of exporting homegrown concepts and methodologies to alien places, where, as we would say today, the "other" lives. As social scientists in the 1950s began doing research in nations newly liberated from colonial rule after World War II, they brought with them the concepts and methodologies they had developed to do political research at home. "I had a sense of mission," wrote Gabriel Almond, the Stanford professor who was soon to become the doyen of comparative politics in the US, "in bringing to the study of foreign political systems the theoretical ferment and methodological innovation which had already gone far in transforming the field of American political studies."[3]

It should not have been surprising or unusual that we came equipped with American concepts and methods to do research in India, among the first of the "new nations." They were what was often referred to at the time as our "tool kit," our means for entering complex and unfamiliar non-Western environments. Without concepts and methods, would we have known where to start, where to look and what to look for. The question was, and still is, to what extent were those concepts and methods amenable to infiltration, adaptation, modification, and transformation by the forms of life and worldview of an alien other? To what extent were the concepts and methods we brought with us from the United States capable of responding to differences between civilizations, cultures, and worldviews? Could they, in the words of Clifford Geertz, "penetrate or be penetrated by another form of life?"[4]

Early in our research in India, we coined the phrase "imperialism of categories."[5] It was meant to designate the academic practice of imposing concepts on the other—the export of concepts as an aspect of hegemonic relationships. Categories crafted in a dominant sociocultural environment are exported to a subordinate one. The imperialism of categories entails an unselfconscious parochialism about categories: scholars from a society taken by its acolytes to be dominant, sometimes called the center, travel to a distant and lesser place, sometimes called the periphery, where they apply "universal" concepts. The trouble is that the concepts have been fashioned out of the center's history, culture and practice—in our case, out of American academic clay.

The title of one of Ashis Nandy's essays, "The Intimate Enemy," conveys the cultural violence associated with the imposition of alien categories. An alien culture, colonial modernism, is unselfconsciously learned and adopted by the colonial other. It becomes part of the other's mentality, his way of thinking and judging.[6] Categories are transferred from the setting in which they were fashioned without regard to their suitability in an alien context.

Categories are also modes of creating and controlling. Foucault showed us how categories embedded in discursive formations,[7] in speech forms, in instruments of sorting, registering, classifying, can function as quotidian modes of power. Ideal-typical dichotomies representing themselves as ways to analyze phenomena in a systematic manner slip into stereotypes. The East is fatalist, says Max Weber; the West, agentic. The non-West conveys status by birth, says Talcott Parsons; the West, by achievement. The non-West is childlike, says John Stuart Mill; the West, mature. Dominant peoples use ideal types and stereotypes to control the dominated.

Feminist scholarship has provided a rich array of stereotypes, especially from nineteenth-century English literature: the hysteria of women versus the sanity of men; the idealism of women versus the realism of men. These dichotomies remind us that effective categories capture enough of reality to make them credible even while they falsify reality in the service of the necessary hierarchies of domination.

Louis Hartz, whose *Liberal Tradition in America* was published in 1955, continues to influence how many Americans think about their nation and history,[8] Hartz did not precisely warn American social scientists that they were unfit to understand foreign societies, but he did observe that Americans in general bore a particularly heavy intellectual burden as they approached the alien other. That burden was a Lockean universalism that taught that the self and the other were the same because they shared a common human nature. The assumption that all persons share a common humanity is one of the normative glories of liberalism. Lockean universalism asserts the equal worth and common reason of all humans. As the Preamble of the US Declaration of Independence put it in 1776, "We hold these truths to be self-evident, that all men are created equal [and] that they are endowed by their Creator with certain unalieanable Rights." But this presumption of sameness obliterates difference when it erases the markers that distinguish cultures and peoples. Survey research concepts and methods *c.* 1957 took for granted that other cultures too were constituted by Lockean individuals.

Writing in *The Liberal Tradition in America*,[9] Louis Hartz explored the negative face of liberalism. He spoke of the moral unanimity arising from Americans' founda-

THE IMPERIALISM OF CATEGORIES

176 tional belief in Lockean universalism, and of their often dangerously irrational devotion to it.[10] Americans imagine the impulses and definitions of their worldview are universal because they take them to be self-evident. Hartz attributed this belief in the self-evidence of rights and reason to American historical experience, an experience epitomized in the quote from Tocqueville that Hartz used to open his book: "The great advantage of the American is that he has arrived at a state of democracy without having to endure a democratic revolution; and that he is born free without having to become so."[11]

The experience of being "born free" means that Americans did not experience radically different ideologies and institutions. They did not have to struggle against feudal oppressions and feudal survivals or the absolutism envisioned by Thomas Hobbes or Robert Filmer. They did not experience the status orders and class differences that shaped Europe's history. Being born free without having to become so produces, in Hartz's view, a complacent liberalism, a liberalism unlike Europe's, which imagines itself as both revolutionary and embattled. According to Hartz, American liberalism lacks the "philosophic spark," the "sense of relativity," the self-consciousness and reflexivity of European liberalism.[12]

Having been born free, Americans assume that the whole world is eager for a similar condition. Hartz argues

DESTINATION INDIA

that the Lockean liberal consensus "elicits an impulse to impose Locke everywhere."[13]

The Empire and Liberalism Suspended

In his *Liberalism and Empire*, Uday Singh Mehta extends the critique of liberalism beyond a parochial American context.[14] He tells us that not only John Locke but also James and John Stuart Mill, both officers in the East India Company, as well as their British compatriots, Jeremy Bentham and Thomas Babington Macaulay, did not confront the anomaly inherent in liberalism's exclusion of entire categories of humanity from doctrines for which they claimed universality. The great flowering of liberalism in nineteenth-century Britain paralleled the great years of the empire. Mehta shows that liberal doctrines were not only made compatible with illiberal colonial rule, but used to justify it. They did so on the basis of a theory of infancy that was used to characterize those portions of humanity that had yet to ascend the maturity-generating evolutionary path that brought the Anglo-Saxon races to their civilized condition: "Childhood is a theme that runs through the writings of British liberals on India with unerring constancy. It is the fixed point underlying the various imperial imperatives of education, forms of Governance, and the alignment with progress."[15]

Nineteenth-century liberalism's understanding of the colonies, like much of twentieth-century modernization theory's understanding of new nations, depended on an historical anthropology of earlier and later that coincided with lower and higher, backward and advanced. A lower position on the historical timeline entails an absence of the capacity to reason which makes deliberation and self-government possible. As John Stuart Mill put it: "Liberty, as a principle, has no application to any state of things anterior to the time when mankind have become capable of being improved by free and equal discussion. Until then, there is nothing for them but implicit obedience to an Akbar or a Charlemagne, if they are so fortunate as to find one."[16]

This theory of historical infancy served nineteenth-century liberalism as the rationalization for and justification of empire. Kipling captured the theory in the phrase, "the white man's burden."

Mehta's countervailing presence to Locke is Edmund Burke. Burke rejected liberal universalism—the doctrine that all humanity is the same everywhere and always. If the universalism and historical evolutionism of nineteenth-century liberals anticipates modernization theory, Burke speaks for the epistemological position of contemporary area scholarship that credits and values difference. He rejects a featureless and abstract liberal universalism for its particular and specific histories and cultures.

Universalist Theory Travels Abroad

We turn now to how liberal universalism assumed the guise of modernization theory. Modernization dominated the comparative politics used in the 1950s and 1960s to analyze and explain post-colonial societies. As a coherent set of concepts, modernization theory has been subject to challenges such as the dependency theory of the 1970s and postcolonial critiques of the 1990s. But modernization theory's central premise and promise, the reproduction of western modernity, endures as a theme in American social science and public policy.

Modernization theory arose out of the structural/ functional systems theory pioneered by Talcott Parsons in Sociology and emulated by David Easton and Gabriel Almond in Political Science. Systems theory's macro, totalizing claims purported to explain all. As Parsons told the Faculty Committee on Behavioralism at Harvard in 1954: "A long-term program of scholarly activity which aims at no less than a unification of theory in all fields of the behavioral sciences is now envisaged."[17]

For modernization theorists, world history moved toward a progressive future. It was driven by an inner reason, or dynamic, that moved in linear, or dialectic, fashion toward a climax represented by the industrialized West.

In this sense the West, and more particularly the United States, was seen to show the nations of the world their future. Modernization theory represented an extension of the liberal historicity we have already discussed—a scientized, objectivized version of the value-laden concepts of James and John Stuart Mill, who viewed the world's peoples as backward/advanced and uncivilized/civilized.

Talcott Parsons' and Edward Shils' pattern variables proved a most seductive way to manage the bourgeoning project of modernization theory. They proposed a series of oppositional dyads to organize the social universe of the modern West and its traditional other: ascription/achievement, affectivity/affective neutrality, collectivity orientation/self-orientation, particularism/universalism, diffuseness/specificity.[18] The items on each side of this dichotomous construction were considered to be systemically related. The left side of the pattern variables represented the traditional world that was to be superseded; the right side, the modern world that was being realized. The teleological cast of the framework mandated movement toward a necessary future. The march of history offered only two possible outcomes: the high road to modernity and the dustbin of history. Nobody drove this agentless process. There was no suggestion of multiple modernities or traditions, much less their mutual penetrations. The

DESTINATION INDIA

Parsons/Shils pattern variables implicitly pitted Anglo-American institutions against those of the developing world and laid out a path by which progress meant the Anglo-Americanization of the colonial other.

The Parsons/Shils paradigm became hegemonic in the social sciences of the later 1950s, 1960s and 1970s. All possible permutations of action could be accounted for: "We maintain," wrote Parsons and Shils, "that there are only five *basic* pattern variables, and that, in the sense that they are all of the pattern variables which derive, they constitute a system."[19]

The systems paradigm profoundly influenced the Committee on Comparative Politics of the US Social Science Research Council, formed in 1954. Gabriel Almond, who chaired the committee, spoke for a broad theoretical consensus when he asserted that the concept of systemic coherence "codified my own implicit paradigm of the interdependence of the components of polities."[20]

Coherence had several implications. If the features of the "modern" system were interlocked and not detachable, "developing" polities or societies had no choice but to buy into the whole basket. There was to be no fashioning of a modernity inflected by particular histories, no picking and choosing, no more or less. Not only were developing societies expected to transition to the predetermined ensemble of Western modernity, but they were also to discard the equally coherent contrasting features into the dustbin of

THE IMPERIALISM OF CATEGORIES

history. Mixed states, hybrids and their occupants, were "transitional," incomplete, and unstable—either on their way to modernity or failures incapable of completing the journey.

Dichotomies are logical structures that suppress the intermediary ground where most of the world exists. Yet it was from intermediary ground that the multiple modernities of Western Europe and East Asia were created. There was nothing uniform about the history of those modernities, no master narrative that explained them all. The factors that led to the modernizations of England, France, Germany, and the United States and Japan were contingently, not systemically, related.

Our quarrel with the dichotomies was that they misunderstood how social change occurred. Most change occurs by adaptation, and incrementally. Particular features of tradition persist, though often modified, into modernity. Tradition is not an unbreakable package; nor is modernity. The components of each are capable of recombination. Individualism may not fully replace collective forms of sociability and action. And despite the depersonalization wrought by modernizing processes, in many societies, group solidarities and other forms of institutionalized affect resist affective neutrality. Particular mixes of timing and circumstance continue to mark the differences among modern societies. Adaptation has enabled a plurality of modernities.

New generations of universalism have washed over modernization theory. Rational choice and globalization bring similar assumptions to analysis. In the social sciences the propensity to imagine that the world is the same everywhere and always is most prominent among economists. When George Stigler and Gary Becker argued in "De Gustibus non est Disputandum"[21] that there were not any theoretically significant differences of taste among human agents, they articulated a liberalism that erased variation.

By the 1980s, formal theory was migrating out of economics into political science in the guise of rational choice. It brought with it the universalism embedded in microeconomics. It also brought with it microeconomics' methodological individualism. It seems that rational individuals are universally motivated to maximize utility.

Rational choice's disdain for the collective and the particular does more violence than did modernization theory to scholarship that aims to distinguish and characterize cultures and societies. Modernization theory at least had a differentiated vocabulary to characterize the other—a vocabulary that recognized alternative social and ideal attributes. Rational choice inquiry and explanation replaces alternative formulations of motive and identity with a uniform, singular concept of utility maximization. According to Amartya Sen, in his article "Rational Fools"

A person is given *one* preference ordering, and when the need arises this is supposed to reflect his interests, represent his welfare, summarize his idea of what should be done, and describe his actual choices and behaviour. Can one preference do all these things? ... Economic theory has been much preoccupied with this rational fool decked in the glory of his *one* all-purpose preference ordering. To make room for the different concepts related to this behaviour we need a more elaborate structure.[22]

Theoretically most relevant to our earlier discussion of Lockean liberalism's universalism is the propensity for formal theory to attribute motives rather than investigate them. The assumption that actors' preferences and choices are determined solely by calculations of rational self-interest is problematic not only because it ignores the role of sentiment, passion, and commitment in behavior,"[23] not only because "rationality" itself is scarce rather than ubiquitous, but also because it is diversely defined by different cultures."[24]

Area Studies as Countermovement

"Area studies" was originally an American bureaucratic construction, an artifact of the cold war. In 1958 the US Congress passed a National Defense Education Act that funded area studies. President Eisenhower and the Congress thought the country needed, among other things, language and area knowledge to carry on the struggle against Communism. Area studies provided a vehicle for 'stockpiling area experts'—a metaphor whose military ring was not accidental.

Area studies legislation and funding and the academic programs that followed suffers from a contradiction. The narrative used to get the National Defense Education Act passed was bellicose; language and area knowledge were needed to defend against the US's cold war enemy, the Soviet Union. But the scholars who entered area studies, with the possible exception of scholars of the Soviet Union, largely brought to the task a benign curiosity and eagerness to understand the other in East, South and South East Asia, the Middle East, Latin America, and Africa.

Academic entrepreneurs were happy to ride the bellicose wave into bigger departmental budgets for esoteric specialties and languages that would not ordinarily be federally funded. Clever deans, collaborating with professors of Sanskrit and Arabic and Chinese, built programs of study and provided for academic appointments and fellowships for enthusiastic scholars eager to spend time among and learn about and from the other.

Area scholars were sometimes accused of being a kind of shadow embassy for the countries they studied. National Security Advisor and Secretary of State, Henry Kissinger advocated the transfer of area specialist foreign service officers out of countries they knew best because, he said, they went native. He was right about that, but wrong about their ability to serve the nation. Their long-term engagement with countries and regions often provided important correctives to presidential decisions driven by electoral or ideological concerns, concerns that detached the president and his entourage from circumstances on the ground.[25]

But area scholars' knowledge of the other and its consequences and implications for US foreign policy rarely effect its conduct of foreign policy. Niall Ferguson, in his book on empire, proposes that the US learn from Britain how to be a global power. America should accept its destiny as a global hegemon and learn how to be an imperial power from the history of the British Empire.[26] Faced with a need to stay the course in foreign lands, America is handicapped, says Ferguson, by Attention Deficit Disorder.[27] It must learn from the experience of the British empire to serve in the spirit of duty and to recognize its civilizing mission.

We don't think that the US should take Ferguson's advice but if it did we doubt that it could fulfill the hegemonic role as he proposes it. In so far as British hegemony worked, it did so because the British accepted and incorporated difference. Britain's feudal past and the royal and aristocratic traces it left in the British mentality and structure of governance enabled the empire to skillfully fit British racism into local patterns of asymmetry, to reward native subalterns by successfully inserting them into the British system of rank and order.[28]

Such cultural suppleness is more difficult for Americans, whose Lockean tradition prevents them from gracefully using difference and inequality to their advantage. Lawrence of Arabia, the double agent of British and Arabian culture, provides a model of British imperial imagination. By contrast, Graham Greene's *Quiet American* (1956), the book that inspired William Lederer's and Eugene Burdicks' *The Ugly American* (1958) depicts the disastrous effects of the American imperial imagination applied abroad. It features Alden Pyle, a CIA operative sent to Vietnam in the 1950s to subvert the Vietminh. Pyle is an innocent who believes that others must surely share his American liberal ideals. His mission ends in disastrous violence. Greene seemed to sense that Vietnam was a tar baby that idealistic Americans would not be able to resist embracing. Pyle's liberal designs to help the natives become more like us captures an American incapacity to imagine the other.

What many area studies scholars had in common with Burke was respect for the dignity, worth, and meaning of the other. That respect could not be enacted except via recognition of the specificity of the other. Area scholars learned to enter into the life of the other, under certain circumstances to "become" the other. They resisted the practice of subsuming the particular *sub specie aeternitatis*, or treating local thought and practice as instances of some abstract universal.

This characterization of the area scholar would hardly have proved credible to the most notable of the power-shapes-knowledge proponents, the late Edward Said. At the time he published his best-known book, *Orientalism*, he believed, in Aijaz Ahmed's effective summary, that "[a]nyone who teaches, writes about, or researches the Orient . . . is an Orientalist ... Orientalism is a Western style for dominating, restructuring and having authority over the 'Orient.'"[29] Despite the fact that Said nuanced his position in subsequent writings,[30] this critique became common among postcolonial writers, both those who lived in the colony and those who lived outside it.

Postcolonial theory bears a complex relationship to area studies. Postcolonial theorists often combine the critical edge of Marxist vocabulary with a respect for cultural determinants that Marx would have disdained. They are as likely to be found in English or comparative literature departments as in the social sciences. Postcolonial scholars disrespect and transgress boundaries. They are "post" colonial in that they attack the justifying prose of imperial and para-imperial authors—and in some cases, such as Ronal Inden, question the capacity of several generations of American scholars of India to present Indians as autonomous actors capable of creating their own social worlds [31] Heirs of Foucault and Said, they lament the cor-

ruption of power and the fatal intermeshing of power and
knowledge. Some see area scholars, especially American
area scholars, as the running dogs of corporate exploita-
tion or an oppressive state. Some, however, see them as
the perspicacious eyes of a postcolonial generation, willing
to pay cultural reparations for the offenses of the western
colonialism and to counter the cultural imperviousness of
an imperial United States.[32]

The language we used above (dignity, respect) suggests
that what is at stake is not just an abstract methodological question, but rather a worldview and commitment.
This is terrain on which area scholars and epistemological
universalists meet and quarrel. Epistemological disputes
in contemporary social sciences remind us that scholars
often invest their chosen modes of inquiry with a moral
aura. At its extreme, area scholars regard methodologies
that do not recognize specificity and context as immoral
because they objectify the other and erase the other's
humanity.

Those who practice such methodologies, the formal
modelers and large-n scholars looking for "data," advocate
what might be characterized as a petrol pump theory of
area scholarship. Area scholars are expected to spend years
and years mastering one or more languages and doing
years of research in "the field," often under adverse circumstances, in order to provide the data sets that modelers and large-n scholars can pump into their formulas and

equations. Their approach toward scholarship is purely utilitarian, exploiting knowledge of the other as the "raw material" of hypothesis testing.[33]

A leading exponent of the petrol pump theory of area scholarship is Robert Bates, an outspoken Harvard professor whose views, if realized, would impose universalism on the other in the guise of "science." "'Social scientists,'", Bates tells us, "seek to identify lawful regularities which ... *must not be context bound* [emphasis supplied] ... [They reject] the presumption that political regularities are area bound."[34]

Yet area scholarship has found itself under attack for inattention to comparative approaches that can generate general theories, especially theories of causality. Hypothesis testers castigate area scholarship for being lost in pointless exchanges about incommensurability, truths of my village versus the truths of your village, exchanges that yield anecdotal specificity but do not produce explanations. A standard area studies defense—that the researcher is exposing the unique qualities of the subject area—is countered by the assertion that even uniqueness depends on comparison.

Area studies is under attack too from another generation of universalists—the globalists, many of whom see regional worlds converging on a single pattern. Some globalists see area approaches as freezing existing regional and national identities instead of examining how those identities are being transformed by global processes. Area studies, they say, emphasizes "relatively immobile aggregates of traits, with more or less durable historical boundaries and with a unity composed of more or less enduring properties." Such static aggregates the new mobility, a mobility which destabilizes the old national and regional objects of research, and attends to the new markers of fluidity: "trade, travel, pilgrimage, warfare, proselytization, colonization, exile and the like."[35] The recent vogue in globalization studies is welcome in so far as it highlights the transnational worlds that state-centric political science and some area scholarship have neglected. But globalization studies often fail to confront the society and politics of the other on the presumption that homogenizing global processes will make "local" knowledge irrelevant. Not yet. Those civilizational and cultural entities that area scholars examine are not going to lose their distinctiveness even when the natives wear jeans, drink Coke, watch television, and surf the Web.[36]

Situated Knowledge

If modernization theory and other universalist schemes, such as formal modeling, large-n studies and rational choice and globalization studies, use concepts and categories fashioned out of the Anglo-American experience and deny difference by not recognizing the autonomy, authenticity, and agency of the other, what epistemology is likely to do so? In our view an alternative to universal knowledge, knowledge that is said to be true everywhere and always, is situated knowledge, knowledge that is shaped by time, place, and circumstance. Situated knowledge proceeds from specificities and works upward and outward to comparative generalizations, rather than downward from a priori assumptions.

We may characterize situated knowledge by the way it makes projections about the future. Universalistic theories project a single history common to mankind, a common developmental path along which all humans will tread. Situated knowledge, by contrast, projects futures by reference to where a culture/society/polity is coming from. Its specificities shape the next step. When Karl Marx noted in the *Eighteenth Brumaire of Louis Napoleon* that "men make their own history, but they do not make it as they please; they do not make it under self-selected circumstances, but under circumstances existing already …," he signaled the limits on historical agency.

The "circumstances existing already" that apply to situated knowledge are of a Burkean sort; they are limits posed by a country's or a people's "ancient constitution."

Despite Marx's caveat that men don't make history as they please, he nevertheless shares modernization theory's projection of a single history for mankind. The way Burke thought of historical agency, positing that futures grow out of pasts, opens the way to multiple histories, multiple paths, multiple modernities, multiple traditions.

We can also characterize situated knowledge by the modes of inquiry it favors. Causality and meaning are at the center of two fundamentally different modes of inquiry. Causality, the relationship between cause and effect—is based on objective knowledge and calls for observation and measurement. Meaning—how humans perceive and understand the world—is based on subjective knowledge and calls for interpretation. The Geertzian questions, If I wink, do I intend to let you in on a conspiracy? Am I trying to seduce you? Have I got sand in my eye? Meaning makes observed behavior intelligible.

Conclusion

The American "impulse to impose Locke everywhere" on a world presumed to be eagerly waiting to receive it has by no means expired. It became starkly evident when America moved toward exporting its liberal values by force. In November 2003 then President George W. Bush told his audience at the National Endowment for Democracy,

> The United States has adopted a new policy, a forward strategy of freedom in the Middle East ... The advance of freedom is the calling of our time; it is the calling of our country. From the Fourteen Points [Woodrow Wilson] to the Four Freedoms [Franklin Roosevelt] to the Speech at

Westminster [Ronald Reagan], America has put our power at the service of principle. We believe that liberty is the design of nature; we believe liberty is the direction of history.[37]

Since Bush's "war of choice" to advance freedom in the Middle East, the US has learned that war—in Iraq, Afghanistan, against Al Qaeda and "terrorism" more generally—does not advance the cause of freedom.

The question is, has America's encounters over the past decade with the "other" in the Middle East and elsewhere in the world, the election of an internal other—an African-American president named Barack Hussein Obama, and its becoming a nation where minorities, an internal other, are becoming the majority, succeeded in giving Americans that "sense of relativity," that "spark of philosophy," that reflexivity, that will enable them to recognize and respect the unfamiliar and the strange it finds in other peoples and cultures? Or will it, as the rise of the Tea Party movement in 2009 suggests, intensify, as it often has in the past, a liberal absolutism frightened of and hostile to difference?

Notes and References

1. Lloyd Rudolph and Susanne Hoeber Rudolph, "Surveys in India: Field Experience in Madras State," *Public Opinion Quarterly* Vol. 22, No. 3 (1958), pp. 235–44.

2. Gabriel A. Almond, *Political Development: Essays in Heuristic Theory* (Boston: Little, Brown, 1970), p. 12.

3. Ibid., p. 11.

4. Clifford Geertz, *Works and Lives: The Anthropologist as Author* (Stanford: Stanford University Press, 1988), p. 5.

5. Lloyd Rudolph and Susanne Hoeber Rudolph, *The Modernity of Tradition: Political Development in India* (Chicago: University of Chicago Press, 1967), p. 7.

6. "This colonialism colonizes minds in addition to bodies and it releases forces within the colonized societies to alter their cultural priorities once for all. In this process, it helps generalize the concept of the modem West from a geographical and temporal entity to a psychological category. The West is now everywhere, within the West and outside; in structures and in minds." Ashis Nandy, *The Intimate Enemy: Loss and Recovery of the Self under Colonialism* (Delhi: Oxford University Press, 1983), p. xi.

7. Power "is both much more and much less than ideology. It is the production of effective instruments for the formation and accumulation of knowledge methods of observation, techniques of registration, procedures for investigation and research, apparatuses of control." Michel Foucault, *Power/Knowledge: Selected Interviews and Other Writings, 1972–1977*, ed. Colin Gordon (New York: Pantheon, 1980), p. 102.

8. James T. Kloppenberg, "In Retrospect: Louis Hartz's 'The Liberal Tradition in America'," *Reviews in American History* Vol. 29, No. 3 (2001), p. 460.

9. Louis Hartz, *The Liberal Tradition in America* (New York: Harcourt, Brace and World, 1955).

10. Ibid., p. 10.

11. Ibid., frontispiece.

12. Ibid., p. 14.

13. Ibid., p. 13.

14. Uday Singh Mehta, *Liberalism and Empire: A Study in Nineteenth-century British Liberal Thought* (Chicago: University of Chicago Press, 1999).

15. Ibid., p. 31. Karuna Mantena in her recent article "On Gandhi's Critique of the State" tells us that Radhakamal Mukherjee

> argued that Western political science, in deeming European history its normative model of political evolution, severely misunderstood the nature and implications of Eastern political formations. Not only was it wrongly assumed that "every race, every people, has traversed in the past or must traverse in the future … the same monotonous road", but any phenomenon that did not conform to the evolutionary model was deemed rudimentary …

Mantena, 2012, p. 554.

16. John Stuart Mill, "On Liberty," in *Three Essays* (Oxford: Oxford University Press, 1975), pp. 15–16, cited in Mehta, *Liberalism*, 70.

17. Harvard Faculty Committee Report, *The Behavioural Sciences at Harvard* (Cambridge: Harvard University, 1954), p. 114. For a discussion of such projects see also Charles Tilly, *Big Structures, Large Processes, Huge Comparisons* (New York: Russell Sage Foundation, 1984).

18. Talcott Parsons and Edward Shils, *Toward a General Theory of Action* (Cambridge: Harvard University Press, 1951), p. 77.

19. Ibid., p. 14.

20. Almond, *Political Development*, 276.

21. George Stigler and Gary S. Becker, "De gustibus non est disputandum," *American Economic Review* Vol. 67, No. 2 (1977), pp. 76–90.

22. Amartya Sen, *Choice, Welfare and Measurement* (Cambridge: MIT Press, 1982), p. 99.

23. For a discussion of the effect of sentiment and passion on rationality assumptions see Jon Elster, "Rational Choice History: A Case of Excessive Ambition," *American Political Science Review* Vol. 94, No. 3 (2000), p. 692.

24. Amitai Etzioni, *The Moral Dimension: Toward a New Economics* (New York: Free Press, 1988), Chapter 8.

25. For an elaboration of this argument and its effects on US foreign policy, see Lloyd Rudolph and Susanne Hoeber Rudolph, *The Regional Imperative: The Administration of US Foreign Policy Towards South Asia Under Presidents Johnson and Nixon* (New Delhi: Concept Publishers, 1980), pp. 23–5.

26. Niall Ferguson, *Empire: The Rise and Demise of the British World Order and the Lessons for Global Power* (New York: Basic Books, 2002).

27. Niall Ferguson, "The End of Power: The Dangers of a World with No One in Charge," *Foreign Policy* (July/August 2004), p. 143.

28. For an overblown version of how the British used hierarchy and theater to govern the empire, see David Cannadine, *Ornamentalism: How the British Saw Their Empire* (New York: Oxford University Press, 2001).

29. Edward Said, *Orientalism* (New York: Pantheon Books, 1978); Aijaz Ahmed, "Between Orientalism and Historicism: Anthropological Knowledge of India," *Studies in History* Vol. 7, No. 1 (1991), pp. 141–2.

30. "The first thing to be done now is more or less to jettison simple causality ... We must not admit any notion, for instance, that proposes to show that Wordsworth, Austen, or

Coleridge, because they wrote before 1857 actually caused the establishment of formal British governmental rule over India after 1857." Edward Said, *Culture and Imperialism* (New York: Vintage Books, 1994), p. 81. Instead, Said moves to a more Foucauldian, "capillary" view of power and knowledge.

31. See for example, Ronald Inden, *Imaging India* (Oxford: Basil Blackwell, 1990).

32. For a report that well reflects some of the ambivalence of postcolonial critics, see Vijay Prashad, "Confronting the Evangelical Imperialists: 'Mr. Kurtz: The Horror, the Horror'," *Samar Magazine* (November 17, 2003).

33. For a discussion of some of the issues see Jih-wen Lin, Gianfranco Pasquino, and Maria Hermínia Tavares de Almeida, "Is There an International Division of Labor in Comparative Political Science?" *APSA-CP Newsletter* Vol. 9, No. 2 (1998), pp. 6–12.

34. Robert Bates, "Area Studies and the Discipline: A Useful Controversy?" *PS: Political Sciences and Politics* Vol. 30, No. 2 (1997), p. 166.

35. The Globalization Project, University of Chicago, 1997. Director, Arjun Appadurai. See also Susanne Hoeber Rudolph and James Piscatori, eds., *Transnational Religion and Fading States* (Boulder, CO: Westview Press, 1997).

36. For one assessment of the persistence among change observed 40 years later, see Clifford Geertz, *After the Fact: Two Countries, Four Decades, One Anthropologist* (Cambridge: Harvard University Press, 1995).

37. The White House, "President Bush Discusses Freedom in Iraq and Middle East: Remarks by the President at the Twentieth Anniversary of the National Endowment of Democracy," United

States Chamber of Commerce, Washington, DC, 2003, http:// 199
www.whitehouse.gov/news/releases/2003/11/20031106-2.html
(accessed on October 10, 1996).

About the Authors

Lloyd and Susanne Rudolph feel at home in three places—Chicago, site of the exemplary University of Chicago where they taught for 34 years; Jaipur, once the capital of an Indian princely state where they have lived off and on for 50 years; and Barnard, a village of 600 in rural Vermont which has been their family home since 1960.

It was the glory days of the South Asia program at the University of Chicago with colleagues such as A.K. Ramanujan, Edward Dimock, Bernard Cohn, McKim Marriott, Wendy Doniger, and Sheldon Pollock. In 1960, while teaching Indian politics and history at Harvard, Lloyd and Susanne bought the house on Silver Lake in Barnard which has been the family home to their three children, Jenny, an assistant professor at the Harvard

Medical School; Amelia, artistic director of Bandaloop, an innovative vertical dance company; and Matthew, who has been teaching about China and India as assistant professor of political science at Georgetown University. During the last three of their 11 research years in India, they went to the Woodstock School in Mussoorie and learned to speak Hindi.

Lloyd and Susanne have loved the great outdoors, trekking in Garhwal, white-water rafting on the Alaknanda, hiking in the Green Mountains and on the Appalachian Trail, and swimming in Silver Lake.

ABOUT THE AUTHORS